THE COMPLETE GUIDE TO
ORIENTEERING
IN NORTH AMERICA

THE COMPLETE GUIDE TO
ORIENTEERING
IN NORTH AMERICA

A COMPREHENSIVE MANUAL FOR THE OUTDOORSMAN

BERNDT BERGLUND

Pagurian Press

DUTTON

Copyright © 1979 PAGURIAN PRESS LIMITED
Suite 1106, 335 Bay Street, Toronto, Canada

A Christopher Ondaatje Publication.

Library of Congress Card Catalog No. 79-50582
ISBN 0-525-03183-9
Printed and bound in Canada

Dedicated
to my wife Clare Elaine
and daughter Kim

CONTENTS

Orienteering builds stamina and endurance, conditions the mind, and sharpens one's powers of observation.

INTRODUCTION

What does the word "orienteering" mean? A part of the Scandinavian languages for a long time, it simply means "navigation on land with the help of a map and a compass."

Orienteering is a great sport, not only for building stamina and endurance, but also for conditioning the mind and sharpening one's powers of observation.

Nature is like an open book, but if you do not know how to read the book it is no good to you, and it can be as hard to learn Nature's alphabet as it was to learn reading from the first grade reader.

Edwin Way Teale, the great American outdoorsman, says, "Nature affects our minds as light affects the photographic emulsion on a film. Some films are more sensitive than others; some minds are more receptive."

The first thing you have to learn in orienteering is to progress slowly. In today's jet age we have grown to depend on all kinds of "instants"—from food to transportation. Unfortunately, in orienteering, there is no instant way. It is a long and rocky road to expertise, with many pitfalls and disappointments in store for the beginner.

Sure, you can say you covered so many miles in so many minutes, but what did you get out of it? How much did you see of the wonders of Nature? Even if you have to slow down to a snail's pace to see them, it will give you an entirely different outlook on life, and the extra time taken is well worth it.

Also, being able to get from one place to another accurately will give you the confidence to get out of a tight spot if you ever get lost in our vast wilderness.

Everyone should know how to use a map. Today we stand at the crossroads in map making. Map-making techniques have taken giant steps in the last decade by the introduction of the metric system of measurement, together with the one thousand meter Universal Transverse Mercator Grid. Consequently, map reading has been given a new slant.

This book will give the present-day orienteer some guidelines to this new system. Consider it a textbook for beginners as well as an update of the excellent work by my friend Bjorn Kjellstrom, *Be Expert with Map and Compass.*

My thanks go to the Department of Energy, Mines, and Resources Canada, without whose help it would have been impossible to complete this book, particularly to L. M. Sebert, head of the mapping program section.

After almost 40 years of orienteering both in Sweden and in Canada, I have written *The Complete Guide to Orienteering in North America* in the hope that my readers will get as much pleasure from orienteering as I do.

The Author

This competitor knows how to get from A to B by the shortest possible route.

If, when looking at a map you feel like the boy riding on the back of a goose and looking down on the earth, you have really mastered the art of map-reading. From Selma Lagerlof's classic The Wonderful Adventures of Nils.

1

THE MAPMAKERS

A long time ago the seafaring merchants around the Mediterranean found that in order to find their way back to lands they had previously discovered they had to keep detailed records. Many of the merchant houses kept these records secret. Written and drawn on rolls of papyrus or pieces of cloth, they were jealously guarded by the merchants, as having or not having them often meant the difference between success and failure for the house. This geographical information became known by the Latin word "mappa," meaning napkin or sheet of cloth, and even today we speak of topographic "sheets." A map was then and is still today a symbolic picture of the earth's surface, drawn to scale on a horizontal projection to which lettering was usually added for identification.

Just as the ancient merchants had different kinds of maps, so do we today.

TOPOGRAPHIC MAPS

The most basic of all is the topographic map. From it a large number of map forms have evolved and have become necessary for the development, administration, and protection of the country.

GENERAL MAPS

General maps are small-scale maps of large areas. These maps range in scale from 1:2,000,000 to 1:250,000, which means that the whole of the U.S. can be represented on a flat piece of paper 14 inches by 17 inches in size.

Many general maps are drawn to show only part of a country, such as a state or a province.

THEMATIC MAPS

Thematic maps are maps with a special theme, such as geological maps, land use maps, agricultural maps, population maps, road maps—to name a few.

All thematic maps are based on topographic maps, but in most cases the topography is subdued so as not to interfere with the depiction of the dominant theme of the map.

NAVIGATIONAL MAPS

The two most important maps in this class are, one, the *hydrographic charts* which are used for navigation on water where the onshore topography is taken from the topographic sheets and the underwater features are taken from hydrographic surveys, and, two, *navigational maps* for air navigation. Small-scale air charts for navigation and approach charts are for use in the vicinity of any major airport in North America.

SPECIAL MAPS

This category includes many, many maps that are almost topographical but don't have sufficient theme treatment to be called thematic maps—for example, maps of national parks and special city maps.

WHO USES MAPS?

Almost every person in North America who can read uses maps in one form or another—road maps for travel along highways and city maps to find streets and addresses. Also, maps are the basic tools for all resource development.

No geological report is complete without a map or a set of maps. The forester notes commercial stands of timber on his map, plots access roads, sawmill sites, possible forest fire control lines, and observation posts.

The hydrologist's interests range from hydro-electric power to irrigation, municipal water supply and dams for flood control.

And, of course, the sportsman or outdoor enthusiast uses the topographical map for scores of activities—orienteering, nature walks, fishing and hunting trips, to name a few.

WHO MAKES MAPS?

In the United States maps are made by the United States Geological Survey and the Corps of Engineers.

In Canada maps are made by the Department of Energy, Mines and Resources, Surveys and Mapping Branch.

WHERE CAN I FIND THE MAP I NEED?

In the United States send a postcard to:
Map Information Office
United States Geological Survey
Washington, D.C. 20242
Ask for a topographic "Map Index Circular" of whatever state you want.

The topographic map is the orienteer's basic tool.

In Canada send a postcard to:
   Map Distribution Office
   Surveys and Mapping Branch
   Department of Energy, Mines and Resources
   Ottawa, Ontario K1A 0E9
Ask for the "Maps of Canada."

Index 1 includes Newfoundland, Nova Scotia, New Brunswick, Prince Edward Island, Quebec, and Ontario.

Index 2 includes Manitoba, Saskatchewan, Alberta, British Columbia, and the Yukon Territory.

Index 3 includes the Northwest Territories.

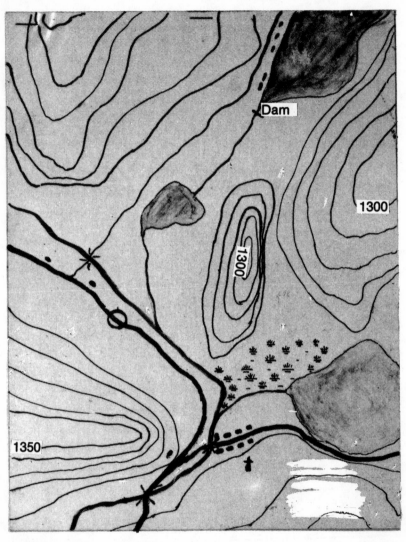

A topographic map showing elevation, man-made, and water features.

2

TOPOGRAPHIC MAPS

Everyone uses a map of one kind or another—a simple drawing to get to a friend's house, a road map, a survey map of a property or cottage lot. These, however, are not suitable for the outdoorsman bent on orienteering, either for sport or recreation. What is needed is a topographic map.

How does a topographic map differ from other maps? A topographic map is a representation of the features of a portion of the surface of the earth, drawn to scale on paper. The features shown on a map may be classified into four main divisions: including seas, lakes, streams, rivers, ponds, marshes, and swamps; including mountains, hills, valleys, cliffs, slopes, and depths; including all the works of man such as cities, towns, villages, buildings, railways, highways, hydro lines, dams, and administrative boundaries; and including wooded areas, orchards, vineyards, and cleared areas. The degree of exactness in representing the features of the area will depend on the relative size of the map to the area mapped.

Lateral Overlap

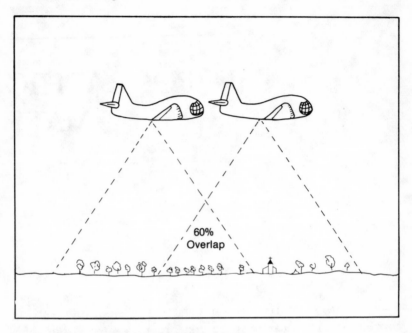

60%
Overlap

HOW ARE TOPOGRAPHIC MAPS MADE?

Before a map is drawn, the area to be represented is photographed from the air, using a special camera installed in an aircraft. The plane then flies at a constant speed and height on a series of parallel strips. An analogy may be drawn between aerial photography for mapping purposes and the act of mowing a lawn—each successive strip of the area to be mapped is covered in the opposite direction to the previous strip. Flight lines are drawn up so that adjacent strips overlap by about 40 percent. Along the flight lines, photographs are taken at intervals frequent enough to allow successive photographs to overlap each other by about 60 percent.

The resulting photos are used by a photogrammetrist (a specialist in making reliable measurements from aerial photographs) to draw the detail to be shown on the map under

Forward Overlap

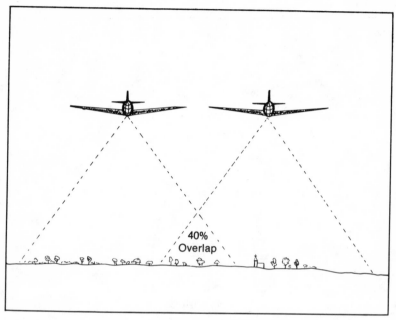

40%
Overlap

preparation. The information taken from air photos is supplemented by additional data collected by surveyors in the field.

The field surveyor first determines the exact location of the maps, its latitude and longitude, and its height above sea level.

THE EARTH'S COORDINATES

The ancient Greeks established a coordinate system dividing the arc between the equator and the poles into 90 parallel circles which get smaller nearer the poles and with the equator as the largest of the parallels. A distance measured along a parallel is called longitude.

Similarly, the equator was divided into 360 parts called meridians, with lines going from pole to pole forming a 180-degree semicircle. A distance measured along a meridian is called latitude.

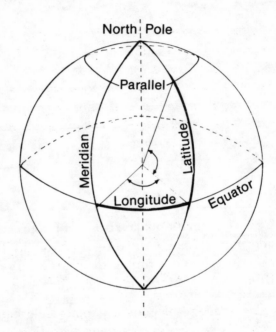

The earth's index system consists of meridians, parallels, and angles of longitude and latitude.

While all the degrees of latitude are equally long (about 69 miles or 42.8 kilometers, or 42,877 meters) the degrees of longitude vary from 69.17 miles (42.9 kilometers or 42,982 meters) at the equator to zero at the poles. The zero meridian or prime meridian lies over Greenwich, England, and the 180th meridian, or the dateline, on the opposite side of the earth. All meridians east of the prime meridian are called easterly meridians; meridians west of the prime meridian are called westerly meridians. The International Dateline is on both the 180 westerly and easterly meridian.

Meridians and parallels are divided into degrees (°), minutes ('), and seconds ("). Each degree is divided into 60 minutes and each minute into 60 seconds.

As we switch over to the metric system it may be of interest to note that one-tenth millionth part of the distance from the equator to the poles, according to international agreement, is considered to be one meter.

PROJECTIONS

Because the earth is a sphere, any representation on a flat piece of paper such as a map cannot be done without stretching or tearing. To do so imposes distortion. If only a small part of the earth's surface is shown, as on a large-scale map, distortion is negligible. But on a small-scale map, such as of maps of a whole country or continent, distortion is considerable.

The map-maker has to decide on a mapping system that best serves the purpose of the map. In other words, not whether to have distortion, but what kind of distortion to have. There are three kinds of distortions: distance, surface, and angle.

Over the centuries various geometrical schemes, known as map projections, have been worked out for representing the curved surface of the earth on a map sheet. All projections have, as we said earlier, certain advantages and disadvantages.

23

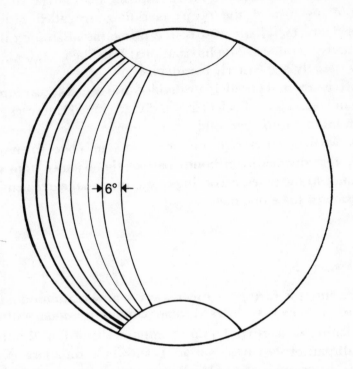

Universal Transverse Mercator Zones

Large countries, such as the United States and Canada, must be divided into strips which are projected onto plans in an orderly fashion. A relatively new system has been introduced into map making in North America called the Transverse Mercator—transverse because the strips run north-south rather than east-west along the equator, as in a Standard Mercator Projection.

A special type of Transverse Mercator is the Universal Transverse Mercator Projection.

To understand how the Projection works, imagine the earth as a grapefruit with all geographical features and the parallels and meridians already drawn in. Now, take a knife and slice off small circles at the poles; then make straight cuts north-south in the skin of the grapefruit and repeat this north-south cut at equal intervals until you have cut off 60 strips.

Each of these strips or zones forms the basis of separate map projections. Envision the flattening by depressing the peel on a flat surface. It is obvious that one could, by using force, flatten the peel until all of it touches the smooth flat surface. This flattening process will, however, distort the peel or it may even break it at the edges. But because the peel is relatively narrow, the distortion is small and may be ignored by most map-makers.

We know that the earth is 360 degrees in circumference. Dividing it into 60 vertical zones gives each zone a width of six degrees of longitude. These zones have been numbered one to 60. Ten of the zones bearing the numbers 10 to 20 cover the United States; sixteen of the zones, bearing the numbers 7 and 22, cover Canada.

After the zones have been flattened into level surfaces, they can be divided into a basic set of maps of a convenient size. These basic sheets are further divided into sections, and each section is published as a map of a larger scale. In the United States and in Canada this is done to produce 1:250,000, 1:125,000, 1:50,000, and 1:25,000 scale maps—various scales of the National Topographic System. By international agreement the edges of most maps fall along parallels and meridians.

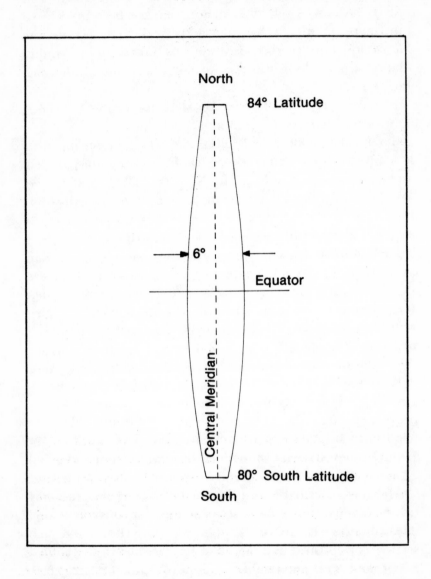

The shape of an individual Universal Transverse Mercator Zone

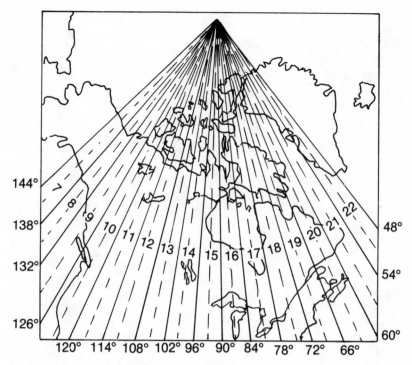

UTM zones and central meridians for northern U.S. and Canada.

Close to the poles, where the zones are narrow, medium and small-scale maps may show parts of more than one zone.

What is important about the Universal Transverse Mercator Projection is that the zones are standard and readily identifiable, so that they may be easily designated as lying within a specific zone.

To make identification and references of geographical features easier, map-makers superimpose a rectangular grid system.

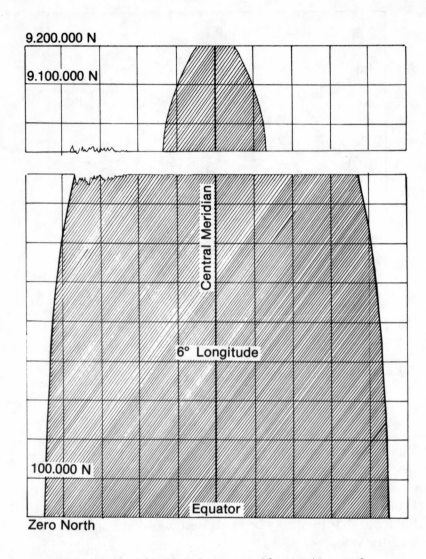

A UTM Zone with 100,000-meter grid superimposed

Everyone has, at one time or another, been forced to locate a street on a city map. Such maps are usually divided by vertical and horizontal grid lines. The grid spaces formed by these lines are designated along one margin by letters, and along the other margin by numbers. A combination of letters and numbers indicates the square formed by, for exampe, the intersecting of column B and row 10, and it is here that the desired street is to be found.

This system works well for a city or road map where the names of streets or cities are clearly printed. On a topographical map, however, where many of the features bear no name, such a system would not work with any precision. Take, for instance, an oil engineer who wishes to pinpoint the location of an oilwell. He would hardly be satisfied with saying the well was located somewhere within an area covering 25 square miles. Military personnel also need a more exact system to be able to pinpoint a place on a map. Requirements such as these led to the development of the rectangular map grid.

The grid system uses as its basic element of identification not squares, as the city map does, but the lines themselves. These lines are standard on all Universal Transverse Mercator maps, and, because the lines are drawn after the grapefruit strips have been flattened, the grid lines are perfectly straight and undistorted. The basic grid lines, both horizontal and vertical, are drawn 100,000 meters or about 62 miles apart.

All vertical lines run parallel to the central meridian of each zone. That is, the meridian that runs down the center of each zone is exactly three degrees of longitude from each side. All horizontal lines run parallel to the equator. Keep in mind that the parallels of latitude shown on our UTM maps are parallel neither to the equator nor to each other because they were slightly distorted during the flattening. The equator itself is not distorted by the Transverse Mercator Projection.

The square formed by the intersection of the 100,000 1-1 meter lines is almost always further subdivided by 10,000-meter lines, 1,000 1-1 meter lines, and even 100-meter lines, depending on the scale and purpose of the map. Most maps show less than the width of a UTM zone, but information is always provided on the margin relating the map to the zone and giving the grid spacing; for example, ONE THOUSAND METER UNIVERSAL TRANSVERSE MERCATOR, GRID ZONE 17.

The wonderful thing about the UTM rectangular grid is that by using a brief code, consisting of zone and grid line numbers, it is possible to identify any point in the United States or Canada, even if that point is not otherwise marked or identified on any map—a feature particularly valuable in search and rescue operations.

HOW TO USE THE GRID SYSTEM

Two systems are in use for identifying points with reference to the rectangular grid. Both are marked on the maps mentioned earlier.

THE CIVILIAN SYSTEM

Horizontal lines are designated by their distance from the equator in meters. For instance, Canada's southernmost point is about 4,620,000 meters from the equator. All horizontal lines in Canada have a "northing" value about that figure. Vertical lines are measured from a center point of each zone, namely an imaginary line lying 500,000 meters west of the zone's central meridian. Actually zones never attain the full width of 1,000,000 meters which such measurements suggest, and in fact in northern Canada, zone widths shrink to as little as 80,000 meters; that is 40,000 meters on either side of the central meridian. In practice, what this means is that vertical lines are counted from the central meridian or the 500,000-meter line. Those to the left of it having an "easting" value of less than

30

500,000 meters, those on the right a value above that.

The number of meters north of the equator on the bottom horizontal grid line on a map is always shown in the lower left-hand corner. Similarly, the number of meters east or west of the zero vertical line is shown in the lower left-hand corner opposite the left vertical grid line.

Where a given point on the map lies exactly at the intersection of a vertical and horizontal line, its location may be read off simply from the map margins. Its full designation or "coordinate" would include the zone number, followed by the easting and northing values.

On a 1,000-meter grid, such a coordinate might read: Zone 17 659000;4986000. The values of the first vertical and horizontal lines appearing in the southwest corner of the map are given in full. The other grid lines are numbered in an abbreviated form.

Very few points, however, are conveniently located at grid intersections. Usually you find that the point described is somewhere between the lines, and it is necessary to measure or estimate the distance to the nearest vertical line to the west and the nearest horizontal line to the south, and add these metric values to the grid values given at the margin. As an example for a point located 400 meters east from the vertical line 357000, and 200 meters north of the horizontal line of 5,476,000, its coordinate would be: Zone 17;357.400-5476200. With these three numbers, any point on the northern hemisphere can be unmistakably identified. There is a similar reference in the southern hemisphere but it is far enough away that confusion never results.

The civilian system of designating UTM grid coordinates is straightforward and, since it uses only numbers, can be handled swiftly by computers and other data-processing systems—a necessity in case of emergency.

It does, however, require using large and somewhat cumbersome figures. To get around this, military map-makers have developed a somewhat different system consisting of a combination of letters and numbers.

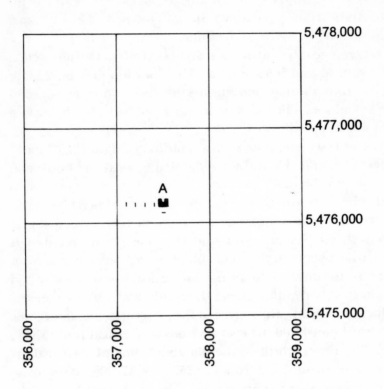

Reading Map References Quickly and Accurately

1. To find reference of building: estimate the number of meters east of 357,000, which is approximately 500 meters. Set it down as 357,500. This is known as Easting.

2. Find the number of the grid line south of the building— 5,476,000. Estimate how far north the building is of this grid line—approximately 200 meters. Set it down as 5,476,200. This is known as Northing.

If there is no possible confusion about the map sheet on which the reference falls, the military system provides a very quick and easy method of referencing. As we have mentioned previously, topographic maps carry a rectangular grid with numbers in the margin identifying horizontal and vertical lines. On large-scale maps of 1:50,000 and larger, each number consists of two digits as shown on page 34.

To arrive at a map reference of the church shown in the figure, we would first note the numbering of the lines that form the west and south of the square. As mathematicians have for centuries given the X coordinate before the Y coordinate, map users follow suit by quoting eastings before northings. Therefore the designation of the square containing the church would be 9194. To give a reference of the church itself we must imagine the square divided into 100 smaller squares (ten by ten). Now we estimate by eye that the church is six-tenths of the way between lines 91 and 92. In the same manner we estimate that it is four-tenths of the way between line 94 and 95. Using these facts we can quote the eastings as being 916 and the northings as 944. By international agreement they are run together into a reference—916944.

Even a higher degree of precision can be obtained by using a Romer scale (a small graduated square).

SCALES

Every map is on a definite size relationship with what it represents. A topographic map must be drawn to a uniform scale to be a true representation of the earth's surface.

All distances on the ground must be shown on the map in the same proportion, and this proportion must be known to the map user. The beginner must obtain a good grasp of this

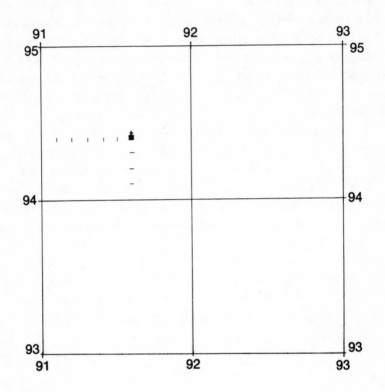

Military Grid

To find map reference of church proceed as follows: Find number of grid line west of the church (91). Ascertain number of tenths to church. The church is east of (91). Estimate that the church is 6/10 east of (91), the number is 91 + 6 or 916. This is known as Easting.

Find number of grid line south of the church (94). Ascertain the number of tenths to church. The church is north of (94), and we estimate it to be 4/10 north of (94), so the number is 94 + 4 or 944. This is known as Northing.

Therefore the map reference of the church is 916944.

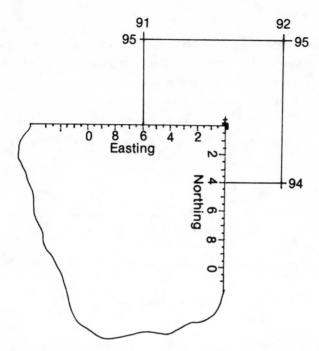

Using a Romer Scale
Read easting first.

subject, otherwise erroneous ideas will be formed in assessing size and distance as shown on his map relative to the actual area on the ground.

There are two methods commonly used to express the scale of a map. The earlier method, formerly used by North American map-makers on topographical maps, was to express on the map in inches, or fractions of an inch, the number of miles represented on the ground. Thus, in the "one inch to a mile" series, one inch on the map represented one mile (63,360 inches) on the ground.

More recently, to conform with international standards, the United States and Canada have adopted the method of showing the scale of a map as the fraction of proportion of map distance to true distance. Thus the 1:250,000 map indicates that one inch on the map represents 250,000 inches, or approximately four miles on the ground.

If all the maps we have were drawn to the same scale it would be an easy matter to compare actual areas on the ground. But all maps are not made for the same purpose and consequently different scales are used.

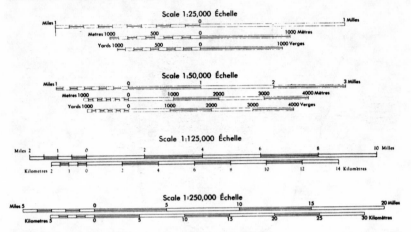

Distance Rulers of Common Map Scales

Maps on a scale of 1:1,000,000 and smaller are called small-scale maps. Maps of the scale 1:250,000, 1:125,000, 1:50,000, and 1:25,000 are called large-scale maps.

Don't let people intimidate you by throwing figures around. Remember that when it comes to scales, the figure 1 is usually used as a base unit. The larger the number below the lines, the smaller the scale. For instance, 1/24,000 means that one unit on your map represents 24,000 units on the ground, but the scale 1/250,000 means that one unit on the map represents 250,000 units on the ground, and, as maps are usually made to the same measurement, 3 feet x 2 feet; a smaller segment of the earth's surface is enclosed in the 1:24,000 scale map than is enclosed in a map of 1:250,000 scale. In other words, more details can be incorporated in the large-scale map. But the area covered in the large-scale map is smaller than in the small-scale map. For example, a jet pilot would have no use for a large-scale map as he would be flying off the map sheet before he could reach for the next sheet.

36

In competitive orienteering, accurate and fast map-reading is essential for success.

37

With today's efficient carrying equipment, a baby is no deterrent to this dedicated orienteer.

And a sportsman looking for a small lake in the wilderness would have little use for the pilot's map in the scale of 1:1,000,000 where the lake would not even be recorded.

Therefore it is absolutely necessary to get a map with the largest scale possible because it will give you more details and features. In the United States a map of 1:24,000 is made up of areas of general public interest and covers about 50 square miles.

The Canadian counterpart is the map 1:25,000 and is available only in heavily populated areas of southern Ontario, Quebec, and a number of regionally important cities across Canada. This series of maps includes coverage of all towns and cities with a population of more than 30,000.

The most common map for orienteering in the United States is the 1:62,500 scale map. An odd number you say—yes indeed, but if you look at it more closely you will see that one inch on the map represents 62,500 inches on the ground or nearly one mile. The mile is 63,360 inches, but this figure is close enough for most purposes, and certainly makes it much easier to use.

The Canadian counterpart is made in the scale of 1:50,000. For many years the Canadian government adhered to the idea of converting this scale into the metric system, where 2 centimeters on the map would be one kilometer or 1,000 meters in the field—a unit often used in the metric system. Today all maps printed in Canada conform to the measure of 1:25,000, 1:50,000, 1:250,000 scale, but the map and survey section still maintains the one inch to the mile scale in cases where the mapping was originally done in this scale.

When reading Canadian maps, you should be aware that maps produced after 1978 have elevation figures given in meters.

MAP SYMBOLS

As it would be physically impossible to carry with you a map which would picture the land in relief depicting mountains, roads, and houses, the map-maker has had to resort to symbols—symbols that can be transferred to a flat piece of paper. To be able to read some of these symbols they have to be enlarged out of scale—buildings on a 1:250,000 map would not be large enough to see with the naked eye, for example.

We discussed earlier the four different features shown on topographic maps: water, relief, culture, and vegetation. On the following pages we will discuss each in turn.

Water

Oceans and lakes are usually marked on the map in blue. Rivers, streams, and canals are also printed in blue. Brooks and

Contour Lines

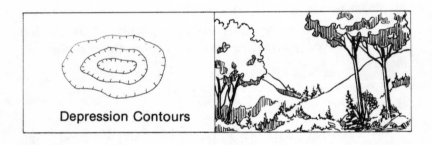

Depression Contours

Cutting

Embankment

small large

Dam

Lake or Pond

large

small

Streams

Spring

Marsh or Swamp

green tint

Wooded Areas

Orchard

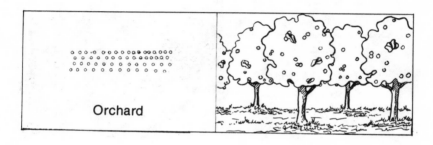

Vineyard

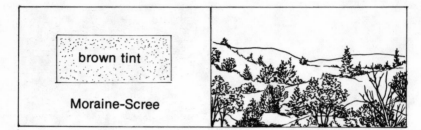

brown tint

Moraine-Scree

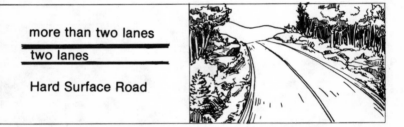

more than two lanes

two lanes

Hard Surface Road

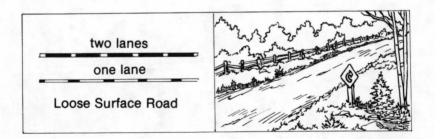

two lanes

one lane

Loose Surface Road

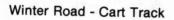

Winter Road - Cart Track

Trail or Portage

Bridge

Footbridge

Ford

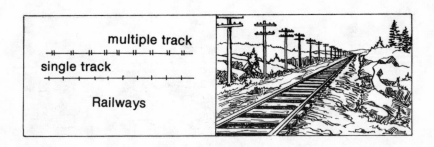

multiple track

single track

Railways

Building   **Barn**

School

Church

47

C

Cemetery

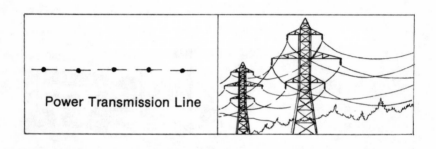

Power Transmission Line

Quarry

Microwave Tower

narrow streams are indicated as a small blue line. A spring is usually marked as a circle with a wiggly tail and a dug well is marked as a circle. Marshes or swamps are indicated as a short line from which topside smaller lines protrude to indicate aquatic growth. Waterfalls are marked as small parallel lines across a river or stream with the letter "F"; rapids are similarly marked, except the letter is changed to an "R."

Relief

The height of the ground in feet above mean sea level is shown by contour lines. For the beginner contour lines are usually hardest to visualize. Think of a contour line as an invisible line that connects points of equal elevation throughout the area presented on the map. The number on the contour line is the height of the line above sea level.

If you were to follow the course of a contour line on the ground, you would go neither uphill nor down but you would remain on the same level. Contour lines are the map maker's way of telling you if the country is hilly, or where it is nearly flat, or where there are indentations or valleys in the earth's surface.

49

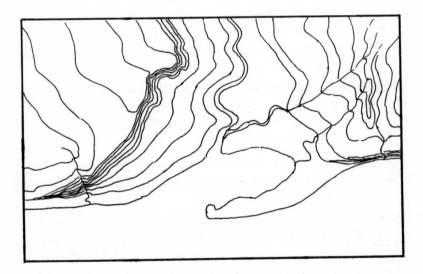

A landscape in perspective, top, and the same landscape, bottom, as it would appear on a topographic map, showing a series of contour lines and the border lines of the lake and rivers. Note how contour lines crowd each other along the cliff.

With the help of contour lines you can determine in which direction rivers and streams flow. Contour lines are printed in brown, with every fifth line marked a little more heavily. If you follow this line you will find a number printed on it that will tell you that every point on this line is so many feet above sea level.

The distance between contour lines is determined by the rise of the land. Contour intervals on a topographic map differ, depending on the part of the land the map depicts. A map showing the prairies, for example, with a contour interval of 5 feet, is usually used because the variations of height above sea level are minimal. But a map showing the Rockies may have contour intervals of 50 feet or more. In each case the number of feet used is given on the map's legend. If the contour lines are close together, it indicates that the land rises steeply; if the lines are far apart it means that the land rises in a gentle slope.

Culture

Culture means everything that has been touched by man's hand. Man-made objects are usually marked on a map in *black*. Examples are roadcuts, buildings, dams or houses, roads, towers, hydro lines, railways. As mentioned earlier man-made features are out of scale, therefore one should measure distance from the center of the symbol.

Vegetation

Vegetation is usually indicated by color. Colors range from white to dark brown. White usually means cleared land or land covered with scrub brush. A light green tint indicates bush or full-grown trees. As the land rises in elevation, the green tint changes first to light brown, finally to dark brown as in the Rockies.

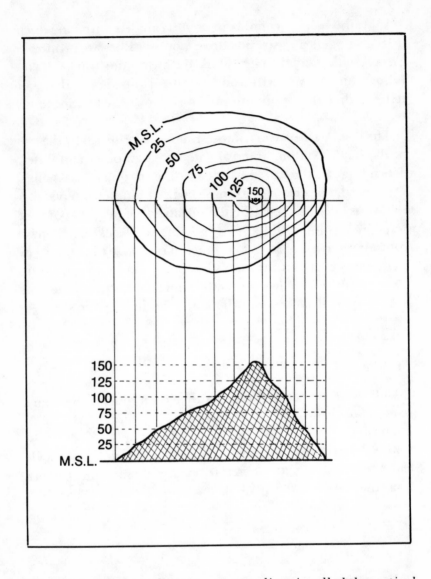

The vertical distance between contour lines is called the vertical interval (V.I.) or contour interval (C.I.); the horizontal distance between contours is called the horizontal equivalent (H.E.). Close contour lines indicate a steep slope; lines that are far apart a gentle slope. Spot heights are heights between contour lines and are shown as 164.

We are now ready to bring out a map and take a good look at it. What can a topographical map tell us? Let's take a walk on pages 54 and 55 around the margin, starting at the top. Here "United States" or "Canada" is printed, which, of course, means the map picture is part of the United States or Canada. In the extreme left top corner is printed 31 E2. This number is the actual map number. Thirty-one refers to square 31 on the National Topographic System. Square 31 is then divided into 16 smaller squares named A, B, C, to P. This particular map is placed in Square E. Each of the small squares is then divided in 16 smaller squares numbered from 1 to 16, and this map is in Square No. 2.

On top of the map on the right we find the scale 1:50,000 and, further to the right, Edition No. 3, and on the extreme right the map number is repeated again.

Starting at the far left lower corner we find the extremely important information about when the map was updated, and how it was updated. In this case the map was updated from aerial photographs taken between 1969 and 1971, and the culture check was done in 1971. It was printed in 1974. (Always look for the most up-to-date map because then you can be reasonably sure that the latest information has been added.) Moving to the right, note that besides the standard map symbols, some new symbols have been added.

Further right, dead center, is our map's name, taken from a main feature which in this case is the name of a small village— "HALIBURTON." Directly underneath is the scale of the map, 1:50,000, and below the scale, the three most common distance rulers are shown. These rulers give you the means to measure the distances on the map either in miles, meters, or yards without having to convert mathematically from one scale to another.

How do you use the scale ruler on a map? First, measure the distance between two points on the map along the side of a piece of paper, then measure against the scale ruler of your

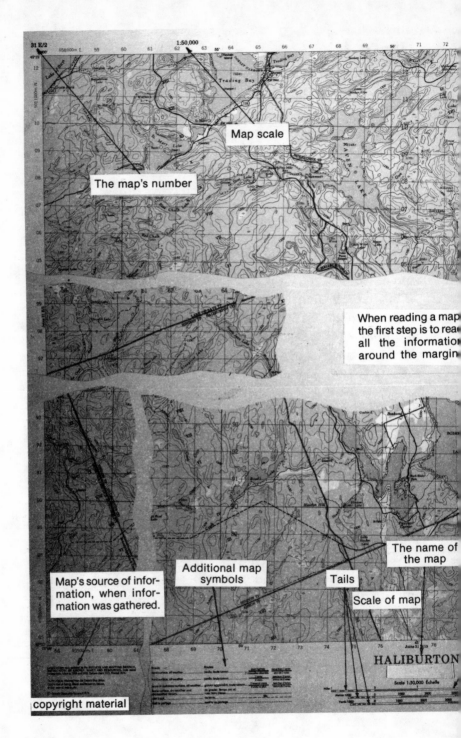

Map scale

The map's number

When reading a map
the first step is to read
all the information
around the margin

Map's source of infor-
mation, when infor-
mation was gathered.

Additional map
symbols

Tails

The name of
the map

Scale of map

HALIBURTON

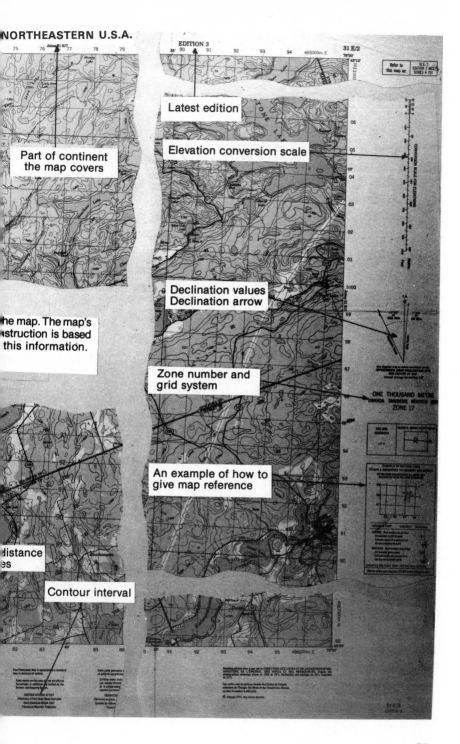

Latest edition

Part of continent the map covers

Elevation conversion scale

Declination values
Declination arrow

he map. The map's
nstruction is based
this information.

Zone number and
grid system

An example of how to
give map reference

distance
es

Contour interval

choice and read off the distance. You will probably not be exact on whole miles, meters, or yards, and now the tail comes in handy. The "tail" is the part of the scale that has been marked off in tenths. Start to the right on a whole measurement and let the measurement come over on the tail (see page 55). As you can see, we have more than one mile but not quite two. By starting at the one-mile mark, however, and going left we have 8 parts on the tail, so the distance will be one and one-eighths of a mile. By using the different scales you can get the measurement in miles, meters, or yards, depending on how accurate you want to be.

To the right of the distance scale is the figure of the contour interval, in this case 50 feet. In the right margin of the map you will find an example of the method used to give a reference to the nearest 100 meters.

On top of the diagram is the description of this particular map "ONE THOUSAND METER UNIVERSAL TRANS-VERSE MERCATOR GRID. ZONE 17."

Above the method of producing this map is a diagram to obtain numerical values of the approximate mean declination for the center of the map. And, finally, above this diagram we have a conversion scale for elevations which converts feet into meters.

We have now wandered all around the map and we have obtained all the information that will be necessary to read the map correctly.

3

THE MAGNETIC COMPASS

The magnetic compass is an instrument with which directions are obtained by the influence of the earth's magnetic field on a magnetized needle, a movable magnet, or a set of magnets (as is the case with the mariner's magnetic compass where a set of magnets is affixed to a compass card that is balanced on a pivot point).

A simplified version of the mariner's compass is the instrument usually used by the surveyor, soldier, or woodsman to determine directions on land. It is the orienteering compass.

While the magnetized needle points in a northerly direction for most parts of the earth, it does not, as a rule, point either toward the magnetic or the geographic pole, but aligns itself along the magnetic field. The origin and behavior of the earth's magnetic field remains one of the unsolved mysteries of science.

The origin of the magnetic compass has not been determined with any certainty. The first ancient seafarers had no compass, and ships on the open sea had to depend on the captain's judgment of the wind and sea. It is believed that the first compass was used in the seventh century B.C., when it was discovered that the loadstone (polarized magnetite Fe_3O_4), a rock found quite commonly around the world, had magnetic properties. But apparently it was not until the ninth century A.D. that it was discovered that a piece of loadstone placed on a piece of bark in a bowl of water would move to indicate direction, and it was not long after that that navigators learned to hang pieces of magnetized metal on a thread or balance them on a needle as a pivot to get an excellent direction finder.

The Vikings were probably the first to use a compass as a navigation instrument, and it is known that Columbus definitely used some sort of compass; it is probably true also that he was the first to discover the variation factor of the compass.

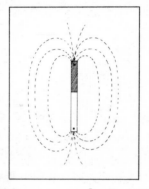

Metal Filings around a Bar Magnet

VARIATION OR DECLINATION

The earth is generally considered to be a huge magnet, with one magnetic pole situated on the northern part of Bathurst Island, Canada, about 77° north latitude and 101° west longitude. The other magnetic pole is in Antarctica. The widespread belief that the compass is controlled by an attractive force centering in one of the magnetic poles is false. The magnetic field of the earth resembles the field which is set up by using a bar magnet under a piece of paper which has been sprinkled with metal filings—an experiment we have all witnessed in school.

The orienteering compass is a simplified version of the mariner's compass. The Vikings were probably the first to use a compass as a navigation instrument.

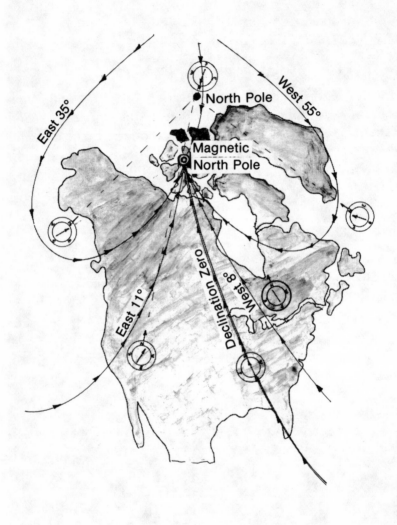

The Earth's Magnetic Field

A magnetized needle or a freely suspended magnet aligns itself along the magnetic lines of force, but since a compass is constructed to rotate horizontally, only the horizontal component of the earth's magnetic lines of force will act upon it. The horizontal component decreases with increased magnetic latitude until it becomes zero at the magnetic poles; therefore in these regions the magnetic compass is rendered useless.

The compass needle points in a northerly direction in most parts of the earth; it does not as a rule point either toward the magnetic pole or the geographic pole. In the United States and Canada it points as much as 30° west on the East Coast and about 30° east on the West Coast. This error is called variation or declination, and a line connecting all points on the earth's surface where the variation is equal, is called an isogonic line. One line connecting all points where there is no variation is called an agonic line. This crooked line crosses the continent from Savannah, Georgia, along the western part of Lake Michigan and up through Lake Nippigon in Canada towards the magnetic pole.

Moreover, the variation is not constant at any given point but changes slowly with time. It is therefore necessary to correct this error in order to obtain a true direction. Another directional error is deviation. Deviation usually results when a small or large body of steel or iron is inserted in the earth's magnetic field, and so bends the natural field. An object such as an automobile, gun, or even a knife will distort the field and give an untrue reading. It is therefore essential to use the compass well away from metal objects. The United States Coast and Geodetic Survey in Washington and the Division of Geomagnetism, Earth's Physics Branch, Department of Energy, Mines and Resources in Ottawa, Canada, periodically publish charts showing values of variation throughout the world.

THE CONSTRUCTION OF THE ORIENTEERING COMPASS

Since the first rough compass of the Vikings, many different types have been used—from the conventional watch-case type

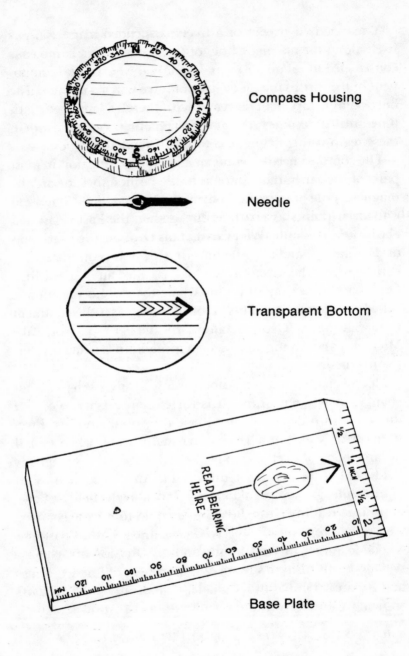

Compass Housing

Needle

Transparent Bottom

Base Plate

The Basic Components of a Modern Orienteering Compass

to the wristwatch or lapel type, plus a variety in between. There is even a compass for the blind, with the Braille system incorporated in it.

But as this book is a handbook for sportsmen we will only talk about the compass most suited to them.

During the many years that I have been orienteering I have never found one that compares with the SILVA compass for durability, simplicity, and accuracy.

The modern orienteering compass consists of three basic parts: the *magnetic needle*, a *revolving compass housing*, and the *base plate*. All three parts work together to form a practical and efficient instrument for navigation on land.

The Magnetic Needle

The needle is made of ionized iron and it is magnetized. Suspended on a needle-sharp point, it swings around freely—horizontally on a sapphire bearing. The north end is pointed as an arrow and is painted red; on some models a luminous point has been added. The needle is submerged in a non-freezable fluid and is completely encased by the compass housing.

Compass Housing

The upper rim is divided into 360 degrees, with the cardinal points marked with the initials N-E-S-W, for North-East-South-West. Each small index line represents 2 degrees and every 20 degrees is marked with a number, 20 to 360. The inside bottom has an arrow engraved pointing directly to the housing's north marking and is called the orienting arrow.

The compass is said to be oriented when the red part of the compass needle lies over the orienting arrow and the compass points in a northerly direction, or when it has aligned itself with the magnetic field at a particular place on earth. Remember, though, that variation figures have to be taken into consideration. Also, in the bottom of the housing are several thin engraved lines running parallel to the orienting arrow, which are, in fact, part of the meridian lines on your map. The compass housing is affixed to the base plate in such a way that it can be turned around freely at the center. To make it easy to turn with cold or wet fingers, the top of the housing has been equipped with a serrated edge.

Base Plate

The base plate is a transparent, rectangular piece of material on which several engravings are made. The main feature is the direction line, which starts at the rim of the compass housing and ends in the direction of travel arrow head. The line at the start also acts as an index pointer to show at what degree number on the housing the compass has been set.

In some compasses two engraved lines running parallel to the direction line and the sides of the compass simplify the reading of the direction of travel.

The front edge of the compass has been made into a ruler graded in inches and fractions of inches. Along one of the sides the base plate has been graded into the metric system, with millimeters and centimeters showing. Both gradations make possible accurate measurement of intended distances along the travel line. In some instances the most common map scales have been engraved.

When all the components have been assembled we have, not only a reliable compass, but a combination of a compass and a protractor. And, believe me, this instrument has not only simplified orienteering but has made it a great sport.

4

HOW TO ORIENT A MAP

A map is a picture of a portion of the earth's surface drawn to scale. But to read a map properly it is imperative that the picture be turned the right way. For instance, you are showing slides of an object and suddenly you have a slide that is turned backwards in the projector. To people who haven't seen the object before, it makes no difference if the house or the people are projected left to right or right to left, but for somebody who knows, it seems all wrong. The same is true of a map. It is absolutely necessary that a map be shown the right way—in other words, the map has to be oriented. *A map is oriented when it is made to correspond with the ground it represents.*

On most maps north is the top of the map. If it is not, usually a large north arrow is superimposed on the map.

There are five ways of setting a map in a north-south direction: by using a compass, by objects, using a watch and the sun, by the stick and shadow method, and by the stars.

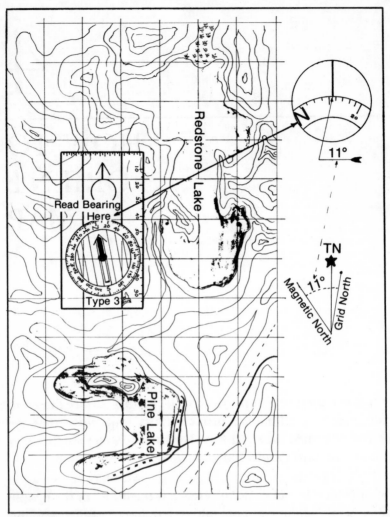

Orienting a Map by Using a Compass

*The margin diagram gives the direction and the size of the angle
between grid north and magnetic north. Do not use the margin
diagram itself as the angles are often exaggerated by the
cartographer so that the number can be inserted. In this case the
difference is 11°. Turn compass housing to 11° as the declination
is westerly, and add. Place compass on map, making sure that the
lines on the baseplate fall over gridlines. Turn the map and
compass until the magnetic needle falls within the arrow. The
map is now oriented.*

66

The declination or variation diagram in the margin of a map will give you the direction and the size of the angles between grid north and magnetic north. Remember not to use the margin diagram itself, as the angles are often exaggerated by the cartographer so that the numerical value of the angle can be inserted. See map on pages 54 and 55.

In this case the angle is 11°. Underneath the diagram the annual change of the magnetic field, which is 1:0′, has been printed. Now go to the extreme lower left corner and see what year the map was printed—in this case 1971. Therefore in 1978 we have an increase of 6 minutes. All we have to do now is: 11° + 6′ = 11°6′. Due north on our compass is 0 or 360°, so we have to add 11°6′ to 0° and set the compass at 11°6′. But how do we know whether to add or subtract the degrees, as there is a westerly and an easterly declination? Well, on our diagram in the margin we can see that the line describing the declination is to the left of our true north line. If the declination line lies to the left or west of the north line we have a westerly declination, which means that the magnetic pole is to the west of the geographical north.

Remember the old saying "west is best and east is least"? What it means is that if the declination is westerly, add the value; if easterly, deduct it. Remember too that the saying has no bearing on the direction in which you are travelling.

As the diagram clearly shows that we have a westerly declination, we add the 11°6′ to the bearing in the compass. Set the compass at 11°6′ and line up the side of the base plate along one of the small blue lines that describe the grid lines; turn the compass and the map until the compass needle lies within the direction arrow.

If the map lacks superimposed grid lines, the value on the diagram usually gives you the angle between the magnetic north and the geographical north. Set the compass as we did before, adding the figures given in the diagram; add the annual change and set the compass. But instead of using the gridlines to line up the compass, use the side or margin of your map, as

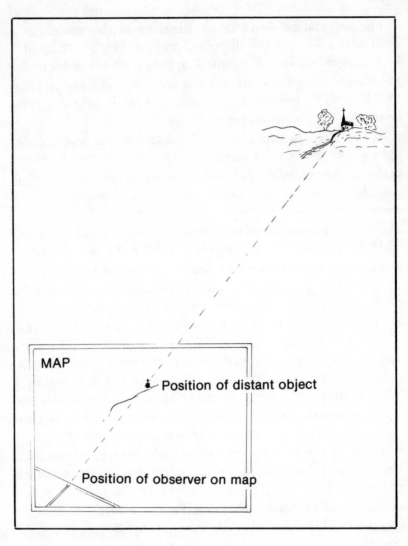

MAP

Position of distant object

Position of observer on map

Orienting a Map by Using Objects

When the observer knows his position on the map and can identify the position of some distant object, he turns his map so that it corresponds to the landscape.

the sides fall along a meridian, and you will get the same result. The map is now oriented toward the geographical north.

OBJECTS

To be able to orient the map by objects, you first have to know your position on the map and you must be able to identify the position of a clearly identified object, such as a steeple of a church or a radio tower. Even the flow of a river or stream can sometimes help pinpoint or orient a map.

Find your position on the map and turn it until it corresponds with the ground.

USING THE WATCH AND SUN

First, change your watch to standard time if it is in effect. The watch has to be as close to the correct time as possible.

Place the watch flat on the ground with the hour hand pointing to the sun. The true north-south line is midway between the hour hand and twelve o'clock. South is on the sun side of the watch. This holds true in the northern hemisphere because the sun never reaches its zenith here, but not directly under the equator. This method is very rough but is useful in an emergency.

STICK AND SHADOW METHOD

Sharpen a stick and jab it into the ground. Try to get it as vertical as possible. Choose a spot that will be clear of shadows from trees or other objects for at least an hour.

Mark the tip of the shadow from the stick with a stone or a smaller stick; wait for at least half an hour and you will see that the shadow has moved. Again, mark the tip of the shadow.

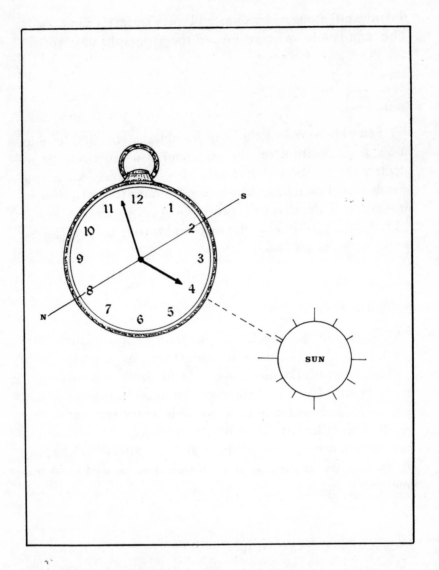

Orienting a Map by Using a Watch and the Sun

If Daylight Saving Time is in effect, set the watch back to Standard Time. Hold the watch flat, with the hour hand pointing to the sun. True south is midway between the hour hand and 12 o'clock. True north is directly opposite. This method will give you a rough direction only; it is not very accurate.

Draw a straight line between the two markings and you will have an easterly-westerly line, with north pointing away from the stick. Again, this holds true if you are in the northern hemisphere and not directly under the equator. Place the bottom of the map along the easterly-westerly line on the ground and you have oriented your map, as the bottom line of the map falls along a parallel. This method is also very rough but serves its purpose.

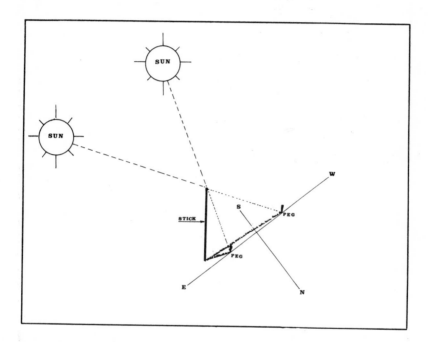

Orienting a Map by the Stick and Shadow Method

Drive a stick into the ground, making sure it is vertical to the ground. Mark the shadow made by the stick with a peg. Wait for 30 minutes or longer; mark the shadow with another peg. Draw a line between the two pegs. The resultant line represents an east-west direction. Another line, at a 90° angle will be a north-south line. (In the northern hemisphere north is always on the shadow side.)

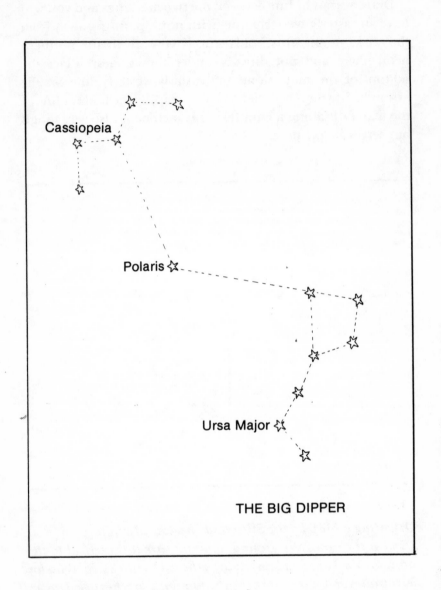

Cassiopeia

Polaris

Ursa Major

THE BIG DIPPER

Orienting a Map by the Stars
In latitudes below 60°N Polaris's bearing is never more than 2°
from true north. Remember that these constellations revolve
anti-clockwide around the North Star.

In latitudes below 60° north, the bearing of *Stella Polaris* is never more than 2° from true north. How can you locate Stella Polaris? First find the Big Dipper, a constellation consisting of seven stars in the northern part of the sky. These seven resemble a dipper, with the last two forming the lip, or, as they are also called, pointers.

Draw a line over the two pointers and extend this line from the lip, then measure the distance between the pointers. Multiply this distance two and a half times along the extension—the Stella Polaris should be at the end of the mark. But remember that these constellations revolve anti-clockwise around the pole.

Make sure that you mark the direction with two sticks stuck into the ground, otherwise you may have forgotten the direction in the morning.

WHAT CAN WE DO WITH A MAP ALONE?

Up to this point we have been talking only about the tools, and not the sport of orienteering, and theory, no matter how interesting, seems to lull one to sleep. But we are now at a point where a little fresh air and exercise are called for. We are like young birds trying out our wings, so don't let us fall out of the nest and hurt ourselves. To become an expert with a map takes hours of practice in familiar surroundings.

We have learned how to orient a map and we already know how to read it. The time has come to take it into the field to compare map symbols with features in real life.

So, starting with a familiar road we will compare our map with what is around us. A good place to start is a clearly marked point, such as a crossroad, school, or bridge. After the map has been oriented, proceed down the road comparing all the features with the map in hand. Obviously the map has to be held so that the top of the map faces north. In other words, if you are travelling in a southerly direction the map has to be read from north to south, or upside down. At first this may slow you down but you will soon learn to read the map in any way. Try a different section of road each time you go out on a new excursion.

Learn, at this early stage, to keep track of distance and how far you have travelled. This is one of the hardest things for the beginner to remember to do because there are so many other things to think of.

How can you measure distances? Distances can be measured in two ways. First, with steps, or, even better, with double steps; second by knowing the time it takes you to cover a distance in various terrains. With a little training, you will have a built-in tape measure with you all the time.

Start with the step method. I am sure that you have often wondered why a mile consists of 5,280 feet—an odd figure. This way of measuring distances goes back to Roman days when, it is said, the Roman soldier of Caesar's time in one thousand paces represented 5,280 times the length of his foot.

The Latin word "millia" was abbreviated into our English mile. But what is a double-step or pace? Count each time you put down your right foot—that is a double step. A double step or pace is approximately 5 feet long.

To get into the rhythm and to find the exact length of your double step, lay out a step-measuring course. Put a stake in the ground, measure off a 200-foot distance, and put another stake in the ground at this point. Walk from stick to stick and back again, counting your double steps. Divide the 400 feet by the number of double steps you took and you will get the average length of your double step.

If you want to practice the metric system as well, remember that one inch is 2.54 cm. In other words, one foot is about 30 cm and therefore 5 feet is about one and a half meters.

Remember, though, that step length varies on uneven terrain. An often overlooked fact is that you take longer steps going uphill than going downhill. (I am still talking about walking, not running.)

The second method is to time yourself travelling in different kinds of terrain.

	WALK		RUN	
	1 MILE	1 Kilometer 1000 Meters	1 MILE	1 Kilometer 1000 Meters
Road & Highway	15 min.	9 min.	10 min.	6 min.
Open Field	25 min.	15 min.	13 min.	8 min.
Open Woods	30 min.	18 min.	16 min.	9½ min.
Mountain & Forest	40 min.	24 min.	22 min.	13 min.

You can estimate how far you have travelled by the time elapsed.

Now, after practice in map-reading and step-measuring along roads, the next step is to try cross-country map-reading. Here it is more important than ever to have your map properly oriented. Never go into the bush unless you have someone experienced with you, or else practice on land that you are thoroughly familiar with. It is very easy to get lost in the bush, so it pays to know the whereabouts of established collecting roads or rivers that will tell you where you are at all times and will bring you back safely if you lose track in the field. And always tell someone where you are going and when you will be back.

Undoubtedly, at some time or other, you are going to experience some difficulties with your map either along the road or in the bush, the most common of which is finding roads, hydro lines, or houses where they should not be—according to your map. Usually it is not that the map makers have forgotten to plot in the features, but that the objects have been added since the map was printed.

Again, I would like to draw your attention to the margin of the map where information regarding the issue year is noted. Very seldom do you get a map that is fresh from the printer,

Orienteering is a thinking sport—mental ability is often more important than physical strength.

therefore changes are bound to happen. This applies particularly to land around large suburban communities where rapid growth often happens overnight.

But it can also happen in far-away, remote places.

In many respects, the desk use of a map is just as important for the sportsman as it is for the planner of a road or pipeline, and you have done your homework properly if when you enter the field for actual map-reading it is like meeting an old friend.

A common fault of the beginner when he or she measures a distance along a curved road or stream is to measure from point A to B in a straight line. The right thing to do is to split up the distance into smaller units and assess each unit separately; in this way you will get almost the true distance.

ESTABLISHING AN ACCURATE COMPASS BEARING

Up to this point we have used established landmarks, such as roads or buildings, but sooner or later we will want to strike out in an unfamiliar direction. To do this successfully we need a protractor. It will establish the accurate compass bearing.

USING THE PROTRACTOR

A protractor is an instrument for measuring angles. Protractors are usually made in a half-moon shape, graduated from zero to 180 degrees. There is also the transparent protractor showing a full circle of 360 degrees, marked zero to 360 degrees, with the cardinal and inter-cardinal markings engraved in the proper positions.

What do we mean by cardinal and inter-cardinal markings? The cardinal markings are the four main directions—north, east, south, and west. The inter-cardinal markings are halfway between the cardinal markings—northeast, southeast, southwest, and northwest. The numbers increase clockwise as you go around the circle.

For instance, north is marked zero, 45 degrees clockwise is northeast, 90 degrees is east, 135 degrees is southeast, 180 degrees is south, 225 degrees is southwest, 270 degrees is west, 315 degrees is northwest, and 360 degrees is the same as zero or north.

An easy way to prove that this is so and learn the degrees is to take a piece of paper about 6″ x 6″ and fold it once. Now you have two of the cardinal directions, namely north and south.

77

Fold it again in quarters and you have created a cross with all the cardinal directions, north, east, south, and west. Fold it again and you have all the cardinal directions as well as the inter-cardinal directions. If you fold it once more into sixteenths you will have the intermediate directions as well. The sixteenths are linked and named by the closest cardinal points—north-north-east, east-north-east, east-south-east, south-south-east, and so on.

The paper protractor is an emergency measure to use in the bush if you are stranded with a watch-type compass and without a proper protractor. Here's what to do: Place the center of the circle over your base camp and line up the north-south line along one of the meridians. Read off the bearing on your estimated travel line. A much more accurate method is, of course, to use a proper protractor where you can read off the degrees much more accurately.

Overall, this is a slow method and success depends on the skill of the operator. Also, you have to depend on two separate pieces of equipment—the watch-type compass and the protractor.

THE MODERN ORIENTEERING COMPASS

A much more accurate way of determining direction is to use a modern compass that combines the two pieces of equipment. As there is only one thing to look after, the risk of losing it is small and accuracy is guaranteed, if it is handled right.

Nevertheless there are five fundamental steps to master. They are:

Step One

Spread your map out in front of you. Establish where you are. This is the basepoint. Find the point to where you want to travel. Join the two points with a straight line. Remember, it does not matter which direction the map is turned as long as the top faces away from you.

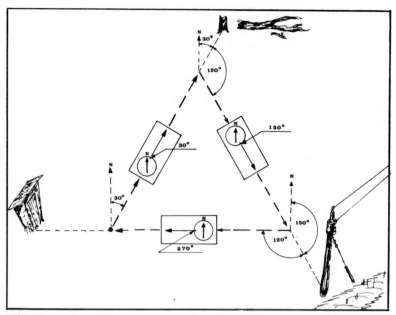

The three-legged compass walk is good practice in learning to use the compass. Use existing landmarks if possible as check points.

Step Two

Place the compass on the map with one of the sides along your travel line, making sure that the direction of the travel arrow points in the direction that you want to travel.

Step Three

Turn the compass housing so that one of the lines on the bottom of the compass housing lines up with a gridline or a meridian line. Make sure that the "N" on the compass housing is towards the top of the map. Some maps have neither gridlines nor meridian lines drawn in on the map. If this is the case you will find index markings along the margin of the map both along the top and bottom. Using a ruler and a pencil, draw a line between the two with the same longitude numbers, making sure that the line runs parallel to the edges of the map.

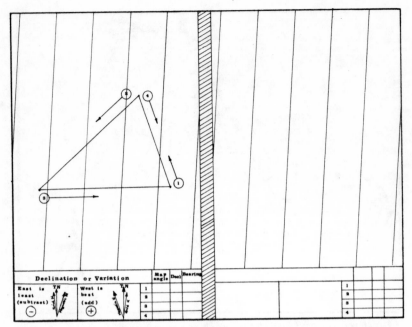

Declination or Variation			Map angle	Dec	Bearing						
East is least (subtract) ⊖		West is best (add) ⊕	1						1		
			2						2		
			3						3		
			4						4		

Sample form used when teaching students how to take bearings and how to properly add or subtract magnetic declination or variation.

Step Four

Read off the bearing on the compass housing where the travel-line starts at the edge of the housing. By consulting the diagram in the margin of the map, find the degree of variation as described on page 67. Add or subtract this figure, as the case may be, from the figure you just read off. Correct the setting of the compass and you will have the true bearing that you need to reach your goal.

Step Five

Hold the compass in front of you. Turn yourself around until the magnetic needle falls within the travel arrow in the bottom of the compass housing. Now, lift the compass to eye level and sight along one of the sides. Pinpoint a checkpoint not more than 50 feet away from you. Proceed up to the check

80

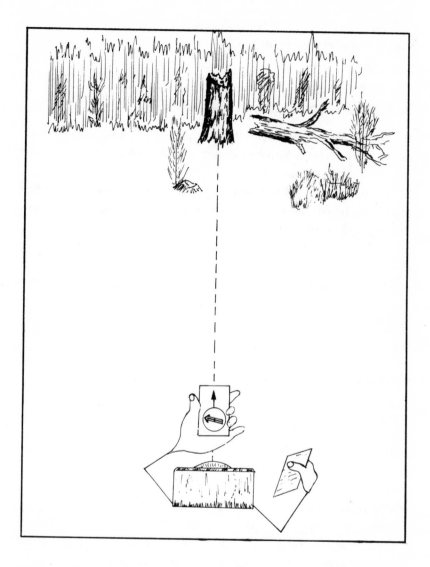

After you have taken your bearing, raise compass to eye level and sight along its side, making sure that you have a prominent landmark directly in your line of travel. Never use as a landmark an object you are unsure of reaching. The distance to the landmark has to be governed by the terrain. In heavy bush you may have to walk from tree to tree in order to keep the bearing.

point, then take another landmark, and, in this manner, cover the whole distance from landmark to landmark until you reach your goal.

HOW TO USE A COMPASS WITHOUT A MAP

A compass *can* be used without the help of a map: one, to find directions, two, to follow a given bearing, and, three, to return to one's original location.

There are many different compasses on the market today, but they can be divided into two main groups: watch-style compasses and compasses based on the Silva system.

Each type when handled by an expert gives satisfactory results, but as we will see using the old watch-style compass is more time consuming and requires a higher degree of skill. But if you have an old-style compass don't despair. With a simple modification you can update this instrument to do an excellent job. The biggest problem is that the housing lacks the benefit of having a stabilizing fluid which slows down the movement of the magnetic needle, and therefore the needle flutters.

To take a bearing or direction to a prominent landmark hold the compass in your hand and face squarely toward the selected landmark. With the other hand turn the compass until the compass needle rests over the north-marking arrow in the housing.

Sight over the center of the compass toward the selected object and read off the number of degrees on the compass housing directly opposite your face. This operation in most cases is not very satisfactory because one cannot depend on its accuracy. But there is a way to improve accuracy.

Cut a piece of medium stiff cardboard about 6″ long and wide enough to comfortably hold the body of the watch-type compass. Cut a hole in the center of the cardboard. Make sure it is a tight fit around the housing. Trim off the ends and cut two "V" slots in each end. Next fold the cardboard one inch from each end. You now have something similar to a gunsight.

82

Again, face the object squarely, holding up the compass and cardboard so that you can sight towards the object in the gunsight. Lower the compass to observe the needle. Turn the compass housing until the needle points towards the north marking. Re-check to ensure you have not moved and lost your landmark. Now fold back the top on the opposite side to your face and read off the degree of bearing in the slot of your "V", making sure that you don't twist the cardboard.

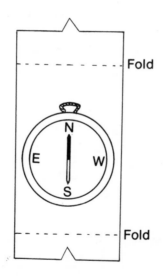

A paper base plate can serve as a temporary base plate for a clock-style compass.

5

THE
A.B.C.'s OF
ORIENTEERING

EQUIPMENT

As with any other sport you need some special equipment. Whether your outing is a Sunday stroll or a competition also makes a difference. The time of year determines how warmly you will dress, but, remember, it is better to have some extra clothing in your packsack than to arrive too warmly dressed. The first requirement for clothing is that it be durable and able to take a lot of abuse. It should be loose fitting but resistant to tearing by branches and other obstructions. A wide-brimmed hat and a pair of safety glasses are musts, also a light poncho and waterproof pants when travelling in the bush late in the fall or in the early morning before the sun has burned off the dew.

A pair of badly fitting shoes can ruin your fun. Running shoes or brand new shoes are no nos at any time. *Boots* should be tall enough to give ample ankle protection—to prevent twisting—and to protect you from scrapes and punctures from stones or fallen branches. Greb's hiking boots are ideal.

Be extremely careful when selecting socks. There must be no binding or chafing. Over the years I have found that a pair of

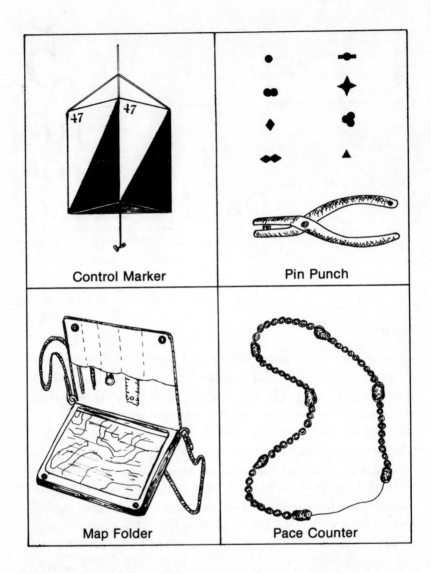

Control Marker   Pin Punch

Map Folder   Pace Counter

Some Tools of the Trade

silk socks underneath wool socks helps prevent blisters. I have seen more than one competition lost because of socks that worked their way down under the soles. Never tuck the legs of your pants inside the shafts of your boots. Usually I wear a pair of short leggings or old army-style *puttees.* In the spring and early summer consider carrying *insect repellent,* as mosquitoes and blackflies can make your outing a living hell. In cooler weather I wear *string net underwear* under a loose fitted jump-suit, a pair of light but durable *high-shaft hiking boots, a light-weight cap* on my head, and I protect my eyes with *clear safety glasses.* I also carry a container of *water.*

Carry a large-scale *topographic map* of the territory, an *orienteering compass,* and a good quality folding, see-through, polyethylene *map-portfolio* into which the map can be inserted. On a wet day this cover will protect your map from damage. The portfolio must also hold a *pencil* and a *scratch pad.* A small lightweight *survival kit* is a must, and I have found a *beadband*—simply a string on which beads have been threaded —to be helpful in keeping track of my paces, should it become necessary to count them.

GOOD MANNERS IN THE BUSH

Remember your good manners in the bush or along the trail. You who have just started this fascinating sport must learn to live up to the high standards set by true outdoorsmen.

Keep in mind the saying, "Leave only your footprints in the grass." Keep your trash and garbage to yourself. You carried in your chocolate bar and sandwich wrappers, and as they are much lighter after you ate the contents, there should be no problem carrying out the empty wrappers.

From time to time you will be in areas where the fire hazard is high. Follow the unwritten law of the orienteer not to smoke enroute. Many states and provinces even have a law which forbids you to smoke when walking or running through the bush. If you have to smoke, sit down where the chances of starting a forest fire are small, and make sure your matches and cigarette butts are always properly drowned.

Sooner or later your bearing will take you close to a farmer's property, maybe even over his fences and into his open fields. Try to find a gate to pass through but remember to leave the gate the way you found it—if closed, close it again, if open leave it open. The farmer had a reason for leaving it the way he did. If no gate is in sight climb the fence close to a fencepost. There you will cause less damage. Never cross a field with a growing crop on it—you will damage the crop. It takes only minutes to go around the edge of the field. Respect *No Trespassing* signs.

Try not to scare livestock. The farmer's property is as precious to him as your front lawn is to you.

AT THE START

Properly equipped and clothed you are eager to begin that first hike. You have arrived at the starting point, you take a quick look at the map, take the bearing, and off you go. Not so fast. The expert orienteer has found from bitter experience that it pays to be systematical and accurate. If you place your starting point or your goal on the wrong spot on your map the whole exercise will be a failure.

Check and double check the two points again and again. Two places on a map can be as alike as twins. When you are sure you are at the right spot for your start and have checked your goal, draw a line between the two points. Also take a good look at the surrounding area. Find a road, a stream, a lake, or other prominent landmark that will act as a catcher's mitt if you miss your goal. This is a good safety rule and will protect you from getting lost in the wilderness. Try to remember which is the shortest way back out in case you have an accident in the bush.

Now, having taken all possible safety precautions, let us go into the details of orienteering.

Clothing must be durable and able to take a lot of abuse.

The first point "A" is the house along the road and the second point "B" is Redstone Dam—a distance of six-tenths of a mile or 1,100 meters. To find the distance take a piece of paper and lay along the travel line, marking off point A to B. Place the paper along the scale at the bottom of the map and you get the distance. (See page 92.)

The next step is to determine the bearing with the help of an orienteering compass. Place the side of the base along the route, making sure that the travel arrow points towards Redstone Dam. Then turn the housing on the compass until the lines in the bottom of the housing are parallel to the grid lines, making sure that the "N" on the compass housing is pointed up toward the top on the map. Now read off the degrees directly opposite the base of the travel line. It reads 68°. Consult the margin of the map to get the declination value. In this case it is 11°42', but as the map was printed in 1974 and the annual change is 0.3' or 3/10 of a minute and the year is 1979, multiply 3/10 by 5;

$$\frac{3 \times 5}{10} = \frac{15}{10} = 15/10 \text{ of a minute.}$$

This gives 12°45' and as the declination is westerly add 12°45' to the 68°. In this case round off the declination to 13 degrees; therefore we have 68° + 13° = 81°. Now reset the bearing to 81° on the compass housing.

Using your pencil and pad mark down this bearing—as a safety measure in case you fall or if the compass housing for any other reason should move in either direction.

The next step is to lay the compass on the flat of your hand, holding it out in front of you and making sure that the back of the compass base is squarely in front of you. Sight along one of the sides or directly over the center of the compass along the travel line toward a clearly discernible landmark not too far ahead of you, a house for example. A quick look around will confirm that it is to your left. As you travel over flat land down to the river side, you will find the river is too wide and too deep

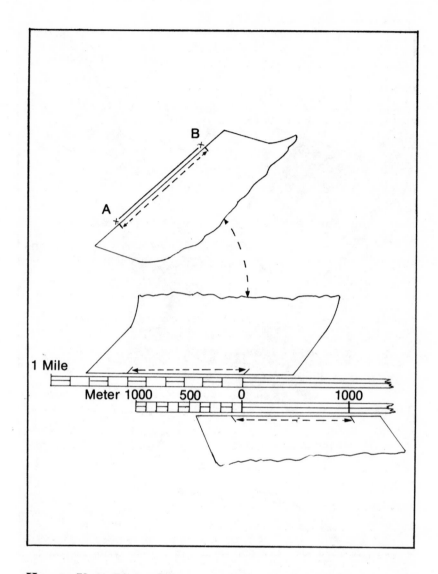

How to Use a Piece of Paper to Find the Distance between Two Points on a Map

Place the paper along the line of travel and mark off points A and B; measure distance on the map's scale, using the tail on the scale. Here the distance is 6/10 of a mile or, using the meter scale, 1,100 meters.

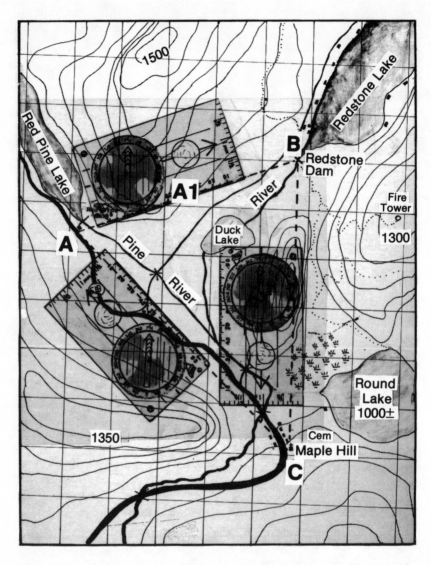

Determining one's bearings with the help of an orienteering compass. See page 90 for a full explanation.

to cross. Take a landmark on the other side of the river. After a look at the map you will see that there is a dam in the river to control the water level in Red Pine Lake and this is a likely place to cross. Walk upstream to the dam and then cross over the river along the walkway on top of the dam. Having crossed safely now walk downstream until you can pick up the landmark you chose from the other side of the river.

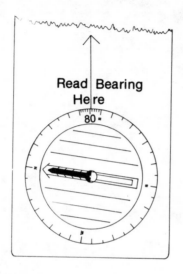

The compass needle should be within the large arrow in the bottom of the compass housing and the bearing should be read under the direction of the travel line—in this case 81°. Remember that there is usually 2° between index lines on a compass.

From here the land should be reasonably flat for about 1/10 of a mile or 150 meters. You will then encounter a rise in the land for about 100 meters. As you cross three contour lines the land rises about 150 feet or 38 meters. Flattening out for about 75 meters it then has a downhill grade for another 100 meters. Next you skirt along a ridge until you see the road running along the ridge. Crossing the road you should see the dam about 50 meters from the road. You have now completed the first part of your hike.

It pays to be systematical and accurate. Utilize all the possible natural features that will help you reach your goal, such as handrails.

The next point "C" is Maple Hill Church approximately 1,400 yards or 1,225 meters away from Redstone Dam. The first thing you have to do is line up the side of the compass along the travel line, making sure that the arrow points in the direction you want to travel. Turn the compass housing until the lines in the bottom of the housing line up along the grid lines. Make sure that the north of the housing is pointing toward the top of the map, then read off the bearing under the travel arrow. It will

94

read 180°. Now add the declination, which is 13° on this map (180° + 13° = 193°). Again you have to place the compass in front of you and line up a landmark.

You will find the first 250 yards or 225 meters to be reasonably flat ground, then the ground starts to rise and it is a steady uphill climb of 250 feet (77 meters) in less than 275 yards (250 meters) until you reach the summit of the hill. After travelling along the summit for 110 yards (100 meters) you start a descent of 250 feet (77 meters) in less than 250 yards (225 meters) until you reach the edge of the swamp. Skirting the edge of the swamp you should see the spire of the church in front of you. Now it is a straight run home, but remember to skirt around or along the farmer's field. *Phew!* It was a hard run in swamp and up and down hills, but we made it! The next goal is to return to the starting point at A. You have two choices. Either take a bearing from point C to A and walk a compass route, or, walk along the highway, which is almost always the easy way out. In the first case, measure the distance by using the paper strip again to get an idea of how long it will take you to get from C to A. (Never leave anything to chance even if it seems to be an easy part of the course.) The distance is 8/10 of a mile (1,400 meters). According to the time diagram it should take you about 13 minutes to travel this distance on the road. You have now completed your first real orienteering course. Do you feel good? You should, if you hit all the controls dead on.

Let's take a look at the course, to see if there is an easy way out. On the first leg from A to B you could follow the first ridge hoping to see the road, or, follow the ridge until A1 and then use the initial bearing. This means you don't have to climb the hill, but it also means you have to either keep track of your time or count your steps. For the second leg from point B to C, you could follow the skid road toward the fire tower, but skid roads can be hard to find. If not often used they are overgrown with small trees and shrubs. This route, however, is the logical one to take; next follow the lower ridge until you by-pass the swamp. Take a southerly bearing which should take you out to the road. Easy isn't it?

BY-PASSING OBSTACLES

On cross-country walks you will often encounter obstacles. A lake, swamp, a hill, or, as in our case, a river too wide and too deep to wade through. It stands to reason that if you can't walk through or over it, you must walk around it. On our course you twice had to by-pass obstacles. The first was easy because you were able to see across it. You were also lucky because you had two prominent landmarks on either side.

The large stone on this side of the river serves as our check point. On the other side the lumber pile, at the foot of a large tree, is another excellent check point. Before taking a new bearing never forget to back check your bearing when on the other side of an obstacle.

In some cases you will not be able to see the other side; you then have to resort to something called "walking around the compass." This is a difficult task for the beginner, but practice will give you expertise. The point of "walking around the compass" is to be able to by-pass an obstacle without changing the compass setting. The by-pass is done by a series of right-angle turns, keeping track of either the number of steps taken or time consumed on each leg. When you reach the point where you decide to start your by-pass, instead of sighting along the travel arrow, sight along the back of the base plate, walk and start counting double steps. If you think you need double steps to clear the obstruction, stop at 200, turn 90° to the left, and again sight along the travel arrow. As you now are travelling in the same direction you were in the beginning, count a safe number of double steps to by-pass the obstruction; in this case 270 double steps. Stop. Make a 90° turn to the left. Now sight along the front of your compass base plate and remember to take the same number of double steps as you had on the first leg, or 200 steps. Theoretically you should be at the same bearing you were on when you started. But remember that the terrain may be different, so estimate or find a landmark to use as a check point. By making a right-hand turn at this point you are on the same travel line as you were to begin with. Simple, but it takes a lot of experience to come out right on this maneuver.

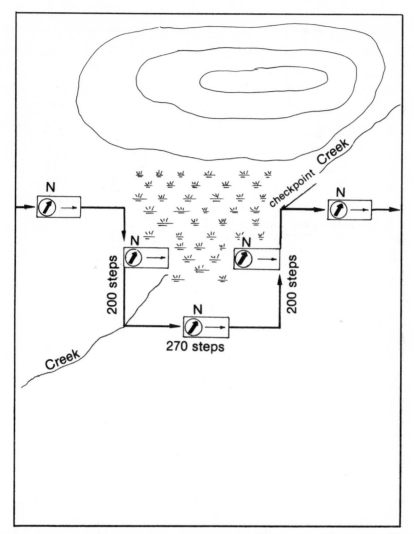

If you cannot see across an obstacle you may have to walk around it. Use the method of walking around your compass, using the back and the front edge of the compass base plate. Never change your bearing, but with the right-angle method and by counting your steps, you should be able to circumvent the obstacle with ease. Remember to check for a prominent landmark on the other side of the obstacle because your step counting may not be all that accurate.

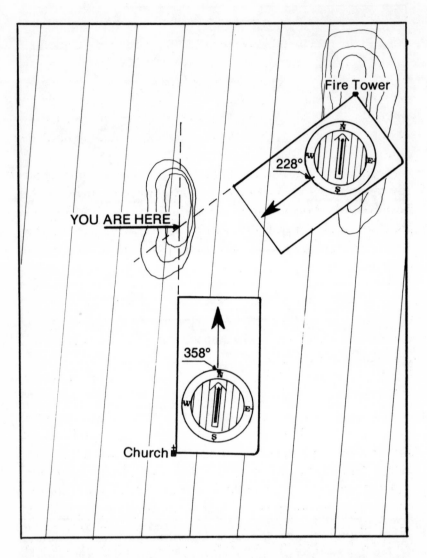

To pinpoint your location, take back readings toward two prominent landmarks—in this case a fire tower and a church. With the landmark symbols on your map as the axis, draw lines from each landmark. You are where the lines cross.

CROSS-BEARINGS

To know how to take cross-bearings can often be a great help in determining exactly where you are. The idea is that you can clearly see and can identify two landmarks on your map. If you take a look at the map on page 92 you can see the fire tower on the hill to your left; if you turn to your right you can see the spire of the church in the village. Take a back reading (hold the compass in the flat of your hand with the compass housing away from you) and line up the side of your compass toward the fire tower. Turn your compass housing until the arrow in the bottom of the housing lines up with the needle, making sure the point of the arrow falls under the north point of the needle. Read the bearing over the direction arrow and write it down.

In this case, it is 215°. To compensate for the magnetic declination on this map, which is 13°W, add 13° and you get a total of 228°. Repeat the operation, but this time take the church as your target. The new figure is 345°; again add 13° to get a total of 358°. Place the map on a flat surface, and set the compass bearing to 228°. Place the compass on the map, with one back corner touching the fire tower. Using the fire tower as the axis, slowly turn your compass without changing the setting until one of the lines in the bottom of the compass housing rests over one of the gridlines on your map. Project a line along the side of your compass in the direction of the travel arrow. Extend the line to ensure that it will be long enough. Take the compass off the map and reset to 358°. This time use the church as your axis and repeat the fire tower operation. Again draw a line along the side of the compass; extend the line until both lines intersect. Where the two lines intersect is exactly where you are.

THE COMPASS WILL SAVE YOU FROM GETTING LOST

Many people get lost during the berry and mushroom-picking season. It is quite easy to do when you are bending over

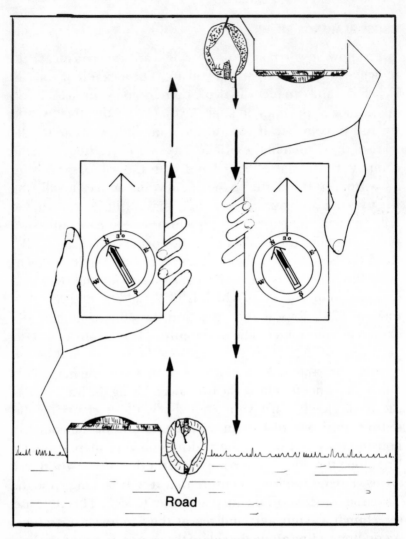

Road

When using a preset bearing to find your way out from a favorite berry picking spot, point the direction of travel arrow towards where you intend to walk. Orient the compass—in other words, turn the compass housing until the needle falls within the large arrow in the bottom of the compass housing. When you want to return to the road, simply pull out your compass, check the setting, and point the direction of travel arrow towards you and start walking.

100

picking berries, because your main interest is to get as many berries as possible, and you go from bush to bush without giving direction any thought at all. Several hours of twisting and turning later it is hard to remember from what direction you came. As you have probably travelled to the picking site on a road of some kind, set your compass before you enter the woods. Here is an easy way to assure your safe return to the base road: put the compass in front of you, with the direction of the travel arrow pointing away from you. Turn the compass housing until the arrow in the bottom of the housing lines up with the compass needle. Read off the bearing and write it down on a piece of paper. Place it in a safe pocket on your person—but not in your jacket pocket which you might take off during the day and perhaps lose. Take a rough bearing in the direction that you are wandering into the bush. When you are ready to leave, check your compass, making sure that the housing has not moved by checking your written figure. The travel arrow pointed away from you going into the bush; to get out in the opposite direction, the travel arrow has to point toward you. This is called backtracking. With this method you can use the same figures going out as you used going into the bush, and you eliminate the risk of making a mathematical error, something that can be quite easily done if you are upset at losing your landmark and the sun has disappeared behind a cloud. You may not come out exactly where you went in, but you will find the road from which you started.

RELOCATING A GOOD FISHING HOLE

All ardent fishermen at one time or another find a spot they want to get back to for more fishing another time—for example an underwater shoal that would be hard to find unless one had a good fix on it. You could of course mark it, but that means somebody else could use your discovery. You can always make a

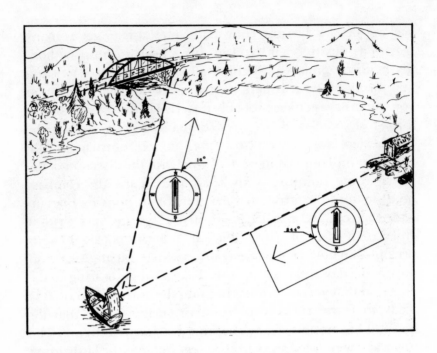

Relocating a Good Fishing Hole by Taking a Cross Bearing

mark on the gunwale of the boat, but unfortunately the mark will move with the boat. The safest way is to take a cross-bearing with your compass.

First, take two landmarks which you are reasonably sure are permanent. A large tree, for instance, may seem as old as time, but a windstorm may change its shape or lightning may make it disappear completely. A house, too, can be torn down or as simple a thing as painting or remodelling may change its appearance beyond recognition.

Take out your compass and place it in your hand, making sure that your metal tackle box, minnow bucket, or rod and reel are a safe distance from the compass. Hold the compass, with the direction of the travel arrow pointing toward you, and sight along the side toward the boathouse and dock from where you came or from where you rented the boat. The travel arrow must point toward you because it will be in this direction you will be travelling the next time you set out to find this spot. Turn the

Orienteering can even be fun for the family pet, who likes nothing better than a romp through the autumn woods.

compass housing until the travel arrow in the bottom of the compass housing falls under the compass needle, arrowhead under arrowhead. Read off the degrees of bearing under the mark. For drawing on page 102 you should get the same bearing as I do—244°. Mark it down and make a clear notation as to what part of the dock you used as the target.

The old iron bridge at the bottom of the bay is another good checkpoint. If the road over the bridge is the only way to get into the boat rental you will know if any alterations have been made on the bridge since the last time you used it. As you have a clear line of sight towards the east abutment of the bridge it will serve as the next check point.

GETTING LOST

Even the most experienced orienteer will at one time or another get lost on the trail. If it happens to you, keep cool; sit down and think things over.

Nothing will drive you into a state of panic faster than doubting your figuring, or disbelieving your compass. Remember—your compass is right 99 percent of the time. What *can* go wrong with your compass? Two things may throw it off. One, a piece of metal carried too close to the compass, and, two, stumbling upon a large iron deposit in the ground. To remedy the former check your pockets—even a cigarette lighter can throw the compass off; to remedy the second simply take 25 or 30 double steps away from the suspected spot.

If you suspect that either of these problems exists, check your calculations. Did you remember to add or subtract the declination? Did you remember to point the direction arrow in the intended direction of travel? Did you turn the compass housing so that the N or north of the housing points toward the top of the map?

Did you study your map carefully enough so that you have clearly in your mind that if you take a direct bearing the catcher's mitt will pick you up? An excellent catcher's mitt is a roadway, river, or large body of water. But first of all never forget to take a back bearing of your compass. In other words, if you travel with the direction of the travel arrow towards you, it should take you back out in the vicinity of your starting point. If you plan to walk into an unfamiliar area, allow yourself

104

twice the time it took you to get there to get back out. Keep in mind that as the day wears on your strength wears out. Also remember that practice makes the expert. Never neglect to practice your orienteering skills. It is fun to discover that through practice you can reach astoundingly accurate results with the help of the map and the compass. And last, but not least, never give up your compass work. Even I, who have orienteered for many years, get into trouble from time to time, but when one sits down to analyze one's mistakes they usually fall into three categories: carelessness in calculation, sloppy execution, or over-confidence. These are the deadly sins of orienteering.

6

COMPETITIVE
ORIENTEERING

Competitive orienteering first took hold in the Scandinavian countries before and during World War II. Backed heavily by the three countries' governments both with money and with qualified instructors, orienteering races became favorite Sunday outings for whole families, and many small towns held both day and night orienteering races.

Today the sport of orienteering has spread to the United States and Canada, and under the aegis of the Orienteering Federation, orienteering clubs have sprouted all over the continent. Outdoor educators have found the different ways and types of competitive orienteering a most satisfactory way of teaching outdoor skills. Competitive orienteering involves not only speed but also smart woodsmanship, a knowledge of map reading, and a sense of keen observation. The sport often attracts individuals who are not necessarily outstanding in track and field, but who nevertheless can obtain astounding results with the help of a map and compass, and so today more and more people are taking up orienteering because of the satisfaction and pleasure they get from taking part in a competitive sport.

Orienteering is a thinking sport, in which mental ability is often more important than physical strength. We all remember the nursery tale about the hare and the tortoise. The moral applies to orienteering—a slow and meticulously planned course will often win over a fast, sloppily planned course.

The basic rules for success are: one, start slowly, two, take plenty of time to check and recheck the printed information, and, three, take time to plan the most advantageous procedure. These rules are just as important for the beginner as for the more experienced orienteer. Naturally, as you become more experienced your speed and accuracy in using map and compass will increase, and you will not only enjoy Mother Nature more and more, but also the camaraderie of the orienteering fraternity.

ORGANIZING AN ORIENTEERING MEET

To organize a successful meet many things have to be considered. First, what time of year is the meet to take place? It makes a lot of difference when laying out the course whether the trees are in leaf or bare—as they are in the late fall or early spring. Remember the controls have to be hidden or else they can be spotted from miles away.

Take the weather into consideration too. If, for example, it has been a wet spring or fall, the course should circumvent large swampy areas and, whenever possible, avoid crossing swollen rivers or streams.

A well-wooded area, preferably with rolling hills and with a ready-made catcher's mitt, is ideal. What is a catcher's mitt? It is

A race is often won because of the keen observational abilities of the participant. Know where on the course you are at all times.

At the start. Read and re-read the instructions regarding the controls until you are sure you have not missed any details.

simply a river or a road or a railroad or a clearing for a hydro line, in other words any landmark that can be used for a safety bearing—large enough that it can't be easily crossed. Some people, particularly beginners, get very upset at getting lost on the course, and the catcher's mitt is their security blanket. But a catcher's mitt is not only for the beginner. It is also important for the experienced orienteer, because an accident can happen to anyone, no matter how careful. A twisted ankle, for example, will make you break off your run in a hurry and get you looking for an easy way out of the bush.

Place controls along readily identifiable natural or man-made landmarks. The following is a selection of commonly used control points:

110

WATER FEATURES

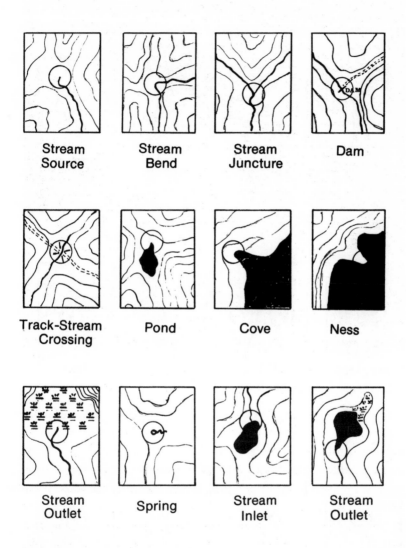

Commonly Used Control Points

MAN-MADE FEATURES

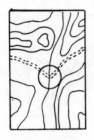 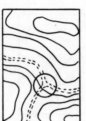 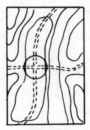 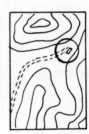

Track Bend	Track Junction	Track Crossing	Track End

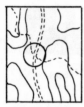 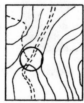 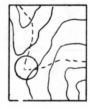 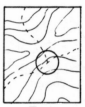

Track-Trail Crossing	Track-Trail Junction	Trail Bend	Trail Junction

 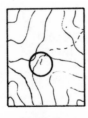 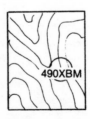 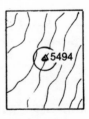

Trail Crossing	Trail End	Bench Mark	Trig Point

ELEVATION FEATURES

   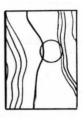

Hill Shoulder   Hill Top   Ridge   Valley Floor

Valley Head   Niche   Knoll   Depression

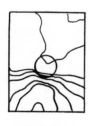  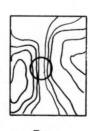 

Valley Foot   Neck   Pass   Hill Side

Remember, too, that the orienteering area shoud be accurately mapped and a recently produced topographical map sheet should be readily available.

Consider to whom the meet is catering—is it for the beginner or the more advanced orienteer? Do not, however, make the beginner's course too easy as it will take the fun out of the competition.

As an organizer make sure you have enough personnel to run off the competition smoothly. You will need registration clerks, starters, track controllers, and safety personnel.

And the last but perhaps the most important consideration is the type of competition you intend to run. Generally speaking, there are two main types of orienteering which, in turn, can be adapted to many other types of competitions.

First, *point-to-point* orienteering. Here the organizers choose the control points in the field and the participant has to plot and lay out the route from one given control point to the next.

Second, *preset-course* orienteering, where the organizers not only pick the control points in the field but also set the route between the control points in advance. The participants have to follow from one unknown control point to another throughout the entire course.

POINT-TO-POINT ORIENTEERING

The three most commonly used variations of point-to-point orienteering are cross-country orienteering, score orienteering, and relay orienteering.

Cross-country orienteering gives the orienteer an opportunity to make quick decisions. To be successful he has to rely on good planning of routes to take between controls, a sound knowledge of map reading, and he has to be accurate in the use of a compass.

Learn from the very first race to stand on your own two feet. Never follow another participant blindly through the bush.

Most national and international championships are held in cross-country orienteering, as it tests the skill of the orienteer to the utmost and is by far the most popular type of competition for this reason.

Score orienteering involves three or more orienteers from the same club, who make up a team. The team usually consists of the three best orienteers of that club, and their final times are added together for the team result.

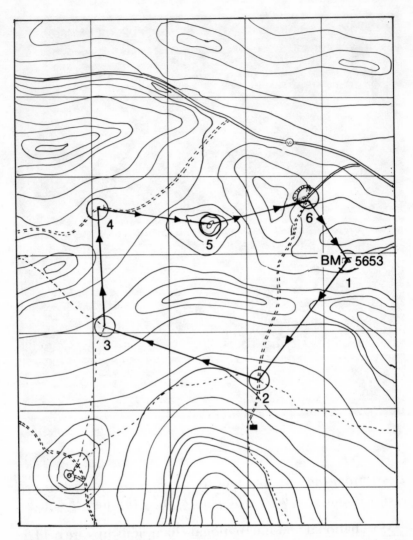

Cross-country orienteering is the most common form of competitive orienteering. Here each participant choses the routes he wants to follow to reach the control points marked on a master map.

Control Descriptions

1. Bench mark
2. Track-trail crossing
3. Trail bend
4. Track bend
5. Hilltop
6. Gravel pit

Relay orienteering is exactly that—each competitor takes on a stretch of the course and a staff or marker is carried from one individual to the next. The marker has to be handed over to the next member of the group at the control points, in the same manner as in track relay running.

CROSS-COUNTRY ORIENTEERING

The cross-country course demands the utmost from each competitor in mental quickness and physical stamina. It also requires great skill in map reading, together with the ability to make quick decisions on how to plot the best possible and the fastest route between controls. When plotting controls organizers of cross-country races should bear in mind that the latest topographical maps must be used at all times—in case some of the landmarks have changed.

There are usually five to seven control points, which should always be readily identifiable by natural or man-made features. The total length of the course should be 8 to 10 miles (12 to 16 kilometers) and the distance between the controls should vary from 600 to 1,500 feet (200 to 500 meters). A course for juniors should be 3 to 4 kilometers long. Ideally the course is a complete circle with the start and the goal in the same spot. A circle is best for participants, as extra clothing and equipment can be left at the starting point and picked up after the meet.

When plotting the course try to give the participants multiple choices in selecting their courses, thus easing traffic over the route. If a great many people participate in the meet and there is only one logical route available, there will soon be a clearly visible trail for the late starters to follow. Take care that the control marker is visible at a distance of a diameter of 90 feet or 30 meters, no more.

Often organizers will produce a special map for the race, but I think it better that you use a standard topographical map in a scale of 1:50,000. The race is, after all, designed to hone one's

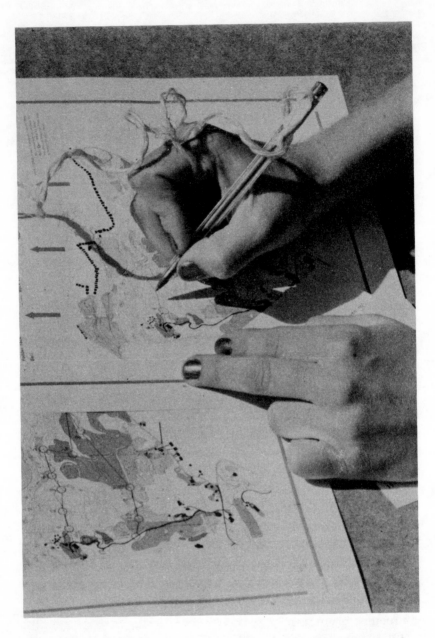

Copy the exact position of the controls on your map from the master map—a quarter of an inch may mean the difference between finding the control or missing it altogether.

knowledge in ordinary map reading, and as the orienteer becomes used to reading standard topographical maps he gains in expertise and confidence. This is, after all, the goal of the exercise.

HOW TO ORGANIZE A CROSS-COUNTRY ORIENTEERING MEET

First, obtain an ordinary topographical map of the area in a scale of 1:50,000.

Check that there are adequate access roads to the starting point and that there is enough parking space. Find a spot where cars can be parked off the road so they will not block traffic.

Make sure the map has a good catcher's mitt for use as a safety bearing. Look for possible check points and routes. If the course at any point goes through private property, get the owner's permission to cross his land. If a lumber operation is in progress within the orienteering area, hold the meet on the day of the week the operation is shut down.

Do not hold a meet during the moose or deer season when hunters will be in the area. This is usually not a big problem as the open season for big game is quite short. The meet can usually be planned around the hunting season.

In the Field

Check parking facilities. Walk the route following the plan. Check natural features against the map, determining check points so that they correspond to the map, making sure that check signs are visible at a proper distance. Obtain permission to cross over private land. Recheck safety bearings, check the supply of local doctors and their office hours, and find one who will be available on the day of the meet. Find out where the nearest hospital is and whether there will be a doctor on duty at times when you might possibly need him.

119

Before the Race

Prepare master maps for each official and assign people to each control. Prepare a description list for each control. Make start and finish signs. Have a table available as a registration desk. Make signs for the catcher's mitt. Organize safety patrols and get instructions down in writing, including how often the safety lines have to be patrolled and what to do in case of an emergency.

Master Maps and Control Descriptions

The race can be conducted in two different ways. First, the participant is given the opportunity to mark down all the controls at the beginning of the race from a prepared master map, and, at the same time, he is given the order in which the controls have to be visited. The controls have to be given a control letter or number and some means has to be provided for the participants to mark their cards, either with a rubber stamp or with a pin punch. (A pin punch is a simple pair of pliers similar to the one a conductor on a train or streetcar uses.) The pins in the pliers, though, must have different symbols.

Second, give the participant only the information he needs to reach the next control. In other words, at the starting point he is given the information where he will find number one. When he reaches control number one the information on how to get to control number two is printed and fastened on the control shield in a waterproof container. In some cases the description has been duplicated on slips of paper so that the participant can remove one slip to take with him—in this case the complete set of description slips can be used as control letters at the goal. No other control system is necessary because if the participant misses one control it is unlikely he will finish, as he has no way of knowing how to reach the next control.

Fasten a check list to the control shield where the participant prints his starting number. When the race is over, collect all the control markers, recover the check lists, and make a final check to see if all the participants visited all the control points—occasionally it does happen that a participant misses one control yet stumbles on the next check point by accident.

SCORE ORIENTEERING

In score orienteering controls don't have to be visited in any specific order, but each control point has been given a score value, the value depending on the distance from the starting point and the difficulties that arise in finding it, as estimated by the organizers. A sound way for the organizers to set the score value is to use a scale of one to 10, depending on the distance—for example, each 110 yards or 100 meters could represent one point. The same scale of one to 10 is used to estimate the difficulties in locating the control. In other words, a control placed at 770 yards or 700 meters has been given the number 7 and the control has been rated as hard to locate—number 10 on the scale. The two numbers are then added and the score value is 17. The score valuation may vary from club to club, but it is wise to decide on a rate ratio and then stick to it, in order to give all the races a consistent value.

When getting ready for this kind of meet organizers lay out the course and prepare the master map in exactly the same way as for cross-country orienteering, except for one thing—the score value is printed in on the master map and description cards. The organizer should keep the controls within an area of about 3 to 4 square miles or 3.8 to 5.4 square kilometers. Lay out anywhere from 20 to 30 controls, making it impossible for any participant to cover them all within a given time limit, usually 90 minutes.

The objective is to reach as many controls as possible within the time limit, and the participant is penalized for any overdraw in time—usually 10 points for each minute. If you

121

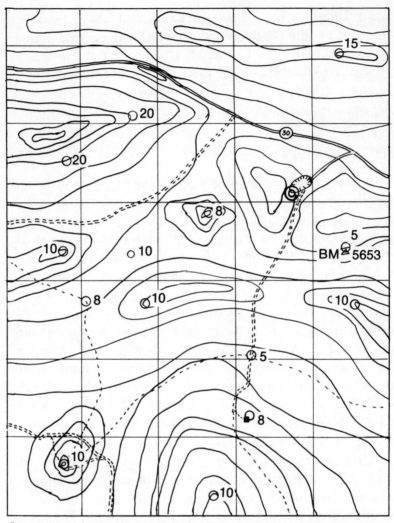

In score orienteering each participant tries to earn as many points as possible by hitting the controls with the highest score value.

Control Values

Bench mark 5	Hilltop 10
Hill shoulder 10	Trail bend 8
Track-trail crossing 5	Ridge 10
Cabin 8	Valley floor 10
Hill shoulder 10	Hilltop 8
	Ridge 15

have a highly competitive field you might have to go to one point for every 10 seconds. Usually, however, this is not necessary.

Score orienteering adapts itself extremely well to team competition where each member works independently, deciding for himself how many controls he can visit. At the end of the meet the total points are added up for each team and divided by the number of participants in the team in order to get the average score points.

Timekeeping starts as the participant leaves the starting gate. The pressure sharpens both his ability to make quick decisions and his skill in deciding on the fastest route to the different controls. It also tests his ability to estimate what he can accomplish within the time limit. Each participant has to leave a card stating how many controls he intends to visit and giving their control number before he leaves the starting point. Each control, of course, has a control number or control letter at the control marker; each competitor is given a control card to be marked as he visits the control points.

RELAY ORIENTEERING

Relay orienteering developed to accommodate team events. By and large relay orienteering is really cross-country orienteering. It can be done in several ways. Here are the two most common:

A team spreads out over the whole course, with one member of each team at each control. A relay staff is handed over from one team member to another at each control point and is carried from start to goal. It is usually a five-control cross-country course. When laying out the course, meet organizers should bear in mind the accessibility of the control points. Ideally team members should be transported to their controls on different routes so that the control points remain as undisturbed as possible.

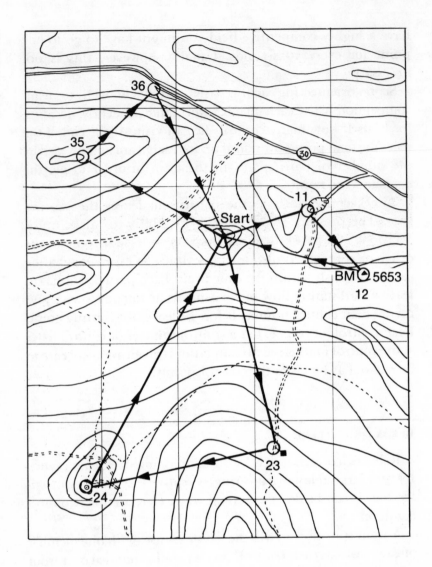

Relay orienteering is a team competition where the team members fan out from a central point which acts as start, goal, and staff exchange point.

Control Descriptions

First Stage	Second Stage	Third Stage
11. Gravel pit	23. Track end	35. Hillside
12. Bench mark	24. Watchtower	36. Road cut

Spend an extra five minutes plotting your course and carefully setting your compass bearing. It will save you valuable time on the course.

This type of relay orienteering limits the number of teams that can participate to a maximum of ten. More than that and the organization becomes unwieldy, as too many people have to be moved around the course.

A better course is a star, clover leaf, or butterfly design. The star can be laid out to accommodate any number of team members, as each member doubles back on each shaft, with start and goal at the same point. If the team consists of three members the clover leaf design is ideal, as each member on the team runs one leaflet of the clover leaf consisting of two or three controls and with the start and goal at the same place. The advantage of this kind of relay orienteering is that the start, the relay-switch, and the goal are in one place, with no movement of people around the course, and it is easy to organize the participants without a lot of track officials.

Here again, control numbers or control letters are used at each control point. The whole team is given access to the master map at the same time; the team is timed from this point on and until the last member of the team arrives at the goal.

PRESET COURSE ORIENTEERING

This is a more leisurely type of orienteering, but it can be as interesting and challenging as point-to-point orienteering. There are two main variations—*line* orienteering and *route* orienteering. The two complement each other and are excellent for initial training in orienteering and for education in the natural sciences.

In line orienteering, the participant follows a continuous line on the master map; in route orienteering he follows a blazed trail and marks in the controls on his map.

Line orienteering gives the participant the opportunity to test his ability to use map and compass along a given route.

Route orienteering, on the other hand, is aimed to sharpen the participant's ability to read a map to the extent that he can pinpoint his location on the map at any point along the route.

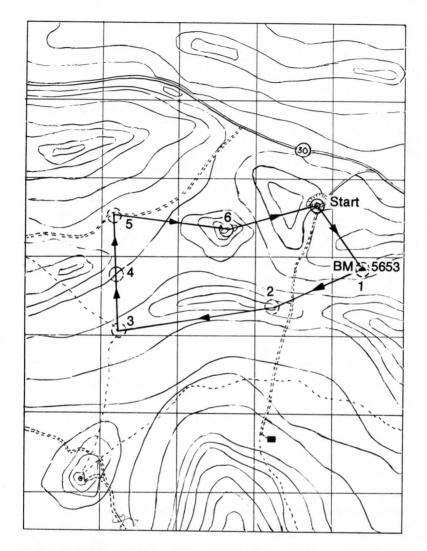

In line orienteering each participant follows a pre-set course drawn on the master map but has to determine and position the controls on his own map.

The length of the course should not exceed 3 miles or 4.8 kilometers, but the course should have many controls—ten to 12 are ideal.

The participants copy the course from a master map which has only a continuous line from start to finish. It is then up to each participant to correctly mark in the controls on his map as he covers the route. The controls are marked with a cross enclosed by a circle. The score calculation is done by simply measuring the distance between the correct position of the control on the map and then where the participant has marked the control on his map. Two fail points are given for each 1/8 of an inch or 2 mm of incorrect distance. In line orienteering neither control numbers nor control letters have to be used.

ROUTE ORIENTEERING

Route orienteering is invaluable for training beginners in map reading and nature lore. The participant follows a marked trail of blazes or streamers; practically no one can get lost.

The master map indicates only where the starting point is. The participant then has to plot in the controls as he proceeds along the course. Marking the controls is done in the same manner as in line orienteering—with a cross enclosed by a circle. The point calculation is also the same.

Many interesting additions can be made. For instance, at control number 1 the participant, in addition to pinpointing the control, has to estimate the distance to three objects in the distance. At control point number 2 he has to plot the bearing to three prominent features in the landscape. At control point number 3 he has to find out how many different species of trees he can spot from that control.

Hundreds of different types of nature assignments can be worked into this type of orienteering to give the orienteer a meaningful and fun-filled outing.

☐ Learn from the very first time on the track to stand on your own two feet. Never follow another participant blindly through the bush. Depend solely on your own observations and your own worked-out bearings. When you first start competitive track it is easy to become blinded by the worship of an orienteering star—if you are lucky or unlucky enough to draw a starting number next to one. Remember, though, that these fellows enter the race to win, and if they feel you are following them, they may deliberately throw you off the track. Keep in mind also that even the expert can make mistakes in selecting the fastest route.

☐ Spend an extra five minutes plotting your course and carefully setting your compass bearing. It will save you valuable time on the course.

☐ Read and reread the instructions regarding the controls until you are sure you have not missed any details. If the instructions have to be copied, write out every single word in longhand.

☐ Copy the exact position of the controls on your map from the master map—a quarter of an inch may mean the difference between finding the control or missing it altogether.

☐ Study the layout of the land in detail. If all the controls are marked on the master map, get an overall picture of the course and plot your expenditure of energy accordingly. Don't be fooled by an apparently easy-to-reach control. A clever course-setter will often have built-in surprises for you. In competition orienteering no control is easy to reach. If the course takes you along trails or roads, make absolutely sure that you have a prominent landscape feature, such as a trail crossing or a knoll, that can be easy to reach and is easily identified.

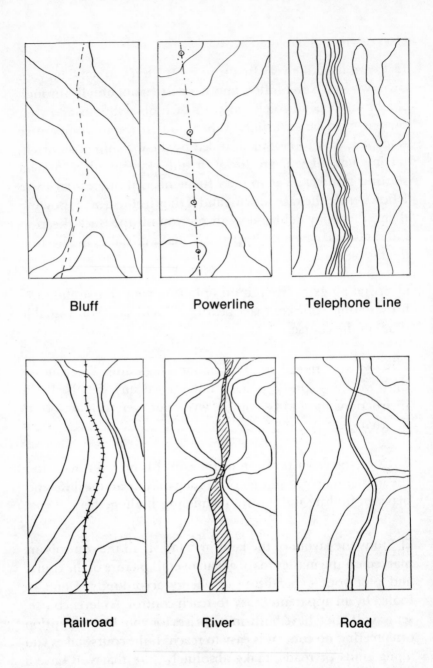

Bluff	Powerline	Telephone Line
Railroad	River	Road

A long feature running more or less parallel to the direction of one's course is called a handrail.

☐ Scout the area backwards from the control on the map to find something that can catch you, in case you miss the intended catch point.

☐ A race is often won because of the keen observational abilities of the participant. Know where on the course you are at all times.

☐ Limit your distance between taking bearings if you are on a strict compass course to no more than 110 yards or 100 meters in open terrain, or you might have to take bearings from tree to tree in dense bush.

☐ Make sure your holding points along the trail are prominent. An object can change in appearance when you get close to it, as sun and shadows make things look different from different angles.

☐ Utilize all the possible natural features that will help you reach your goal, such as handrails. In the language of the orienteer a handrail is a long feature that runs more or less parallel to the course—for example, a power line, hydro line, and a fence are perfect handrails.

☐ Beware of taking bearings with your compass under a hydro line. The magnetic field surrounding the hydro line might throw your compass off. The same goes for a metal fence or a line of barbed wire. Some track-setters just love to place a control marker close to a metal fence just to see if you are observant enough to go away from the fence when taking the new bearing.

☐ A fast-moving stream is better than a slow-moving stream as a handrail. The fast-moving stream is more apt to flow in a straight line; the slower stream will wind its way down through the landscape and will lengthen the distance you have to travel. It can also throw you off the bearing.

☐ When choosing a route consider choosing one with many prominent check points even if it is slightly longer.

☐ Opposite the handrail is the cross check, a feature in nature that crosses your route—a hydro line, a road, or a ridge serves the purpose providing it runs at a 90-degree angle to your route.

☐ The shortest distance between two points is a straight line. In orienteering, however, this is not always true. For instance, the line might run over a steep hill, and remember you are looking at the line three dimensionally. The actual length over the hill might be longer than if you had circumvented the hill, even if this line is crooked. By the same token it will take a lot of energy to climb the hill—energy you can ill afford to lose. It may be better to follow the contour line on a lower level or walk around your compass, counting your steps.

☐ It is a good idea to make a bead band for this purpose. Take a string and thread on some beads, with every tenth bead a different color. This device will help you keep track of how many double steps you have taken. Sometimes it is hard to keep track of the steps if the going gets tough. For many years I used a nylon line strung with dried yellow peas; as a divider every tenth bead was brown.

☐ Never under any circumstances cross a swamp, bog, pond, lake, newly planted field, or field with growing crops. If you can see across the obstacle, take a good check point on the opposite side, then run around it and pick up the trail on the other side. Now take a compass bearing and continue the race.

When choosing a route consider one with many check points, even if it is the slightly longer way.

The actual placing of the control points depends on what class of orienteer you are catering to—obscure and hard-to-find control points for the experts, more prominent points for the less experienced.

☐ Check your map against the master map to make sure you have the same edition. Any map over a district will not do, as a later edition of the map undoubtedly will contain differences that will throw you off.

☐ Do not forget to compensate for the declination after having plotted the course. Always make sure that the declination figures or the declination arrow tell you the exact declination value. The declination figures are usually given for the center of the mapsheet. On maps covering the northern part of the continent the declination may change from one side of the map to the other (particularly as most maps of the northern part of North America are in the scale of 1:250,000).

☐ Beware of the new maps with the grid system superimposed on the maps, if the declination value is calibrated to the grid lines or to the meridian lines.

☐ Divide your course into three segments, depending on where you are: green, for going all out; yellow, caution has to be exercised; red, stop and think. We have been trained to obey these signals on street corners. Now it is time to train yourself to obey them on the course.

☐ In the green sector, the rough orienteering method can be used. This means you follow a road or a natural feature until you reach a holding point. Neither an exact compass reading nor a detailed map study is needed but it is important that you can locate yourself at any moment along the route.

The yellow caution sector is necessary in order that you do not over-run the checkpoint. After reaching the yellow sector make closer and more frequent checks of your map and compass and take closer aiming points. The run in from the last holding point to the control is the red sector which requires exact, precision orienteering—close checks of the compass bearing and exact map reading—until you reach the control point.

THE GREEN SECTOR

Hold the compass in front of you and turn your body until the compass needle falls into the arrow in the bottom of the compass housing. (Learn to turn your body by using small movements of your feet, not by pivoting the upper part of your body, as you will have a tendency to swing back in the direction that your feet are pointing.)

Take an aiming point directly in line with the travel arrow, not too far away but also not too close—after all you may have the handrail to hang on to. When you reach the aiming point repeat the operation and take another aiming point. Repeat as often as you think necessary.

After you have determined an aiming point, let the compass hang on the string. Do this every time. In the beginning you will have a tendency to walk with the compass in front of you all the time, but beware of this practice as it will get you into a bad habit. Also, it is dangerous as you cannot see where you are putting your feet. Any obstruction on the ground will trip you. From time to time check your handrail and move your thumb along your route on the map.

Have I told you about using your thumb as a movable marker? As you go along the route and reach your check points, simply move your thumb from check point to check point and you will always know where you are on the map. Some people call it "map-reading-by-thumb."

Always keep your map oriented—the north on the map in a northerly direction, even if it means you have to read the map upside down or sideways. If you don't do this, features in nature will not correspond to the map.

When you get close to your last cross-check point and the end of the green sector, the yellow light should flash on in your mind.

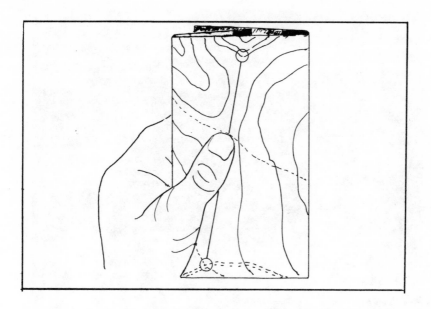

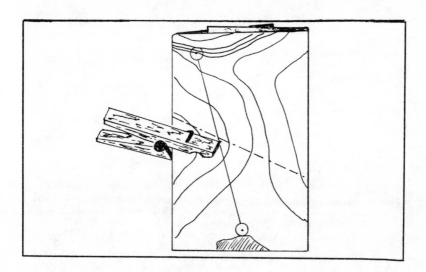

Often orienteers use their thumbs to follow their progress on maps. For greater accuracy, use a clothespin to mark where you are.

A control should never be found by chance, but should depend solely on the skill of the orienteer.

THE YELLOW SECTOR

The yellow signal warns you that the time has come for more careful map-reading and that a close check of your compass bearing has to be maintained.

Carefully check all natural features to make sure they correspond to the map and that the handrail has not taken you too far off the course. Remember, too, that if you are following a trail the trail may have changed direction since the map was printed. To be sure of distances between check points you may have to bring out your beads and resort to counting double steps to keep track of your travelled distance. You cannot afford to miss a cross check point now. Use the side of your orienteering compass with the engraved inch or centimeter rule to determine the distances on the map. Remember when pacing that a person usually takes a longer step uphill than downhill, which is when he puts on the brakes. (It is important to have previously tested and know the length of your pace in different kinds of terrain.)

THE RED SECTOR

The last part of your course into the control marker is the most critical. Exercise utmost caution in the red sector. Minute, detailed map reading is necessary as well as careful setting of your compass bearings. (Don't forget the declination.)

Very short aiming distances are a must. It is time-consuming but you will soon find out that it is more time-consuming to have to retrace your steps to the last check point and start again.

When you do reach the control marker read the description of the next control very carefully before you start plotting the new course, and don't forget to mark your control card with the correct control number or letter, whichever is the case. Many a race has been lost because the orienteer forgot to mark this important information on his card.

The success of the meet or race depends largely on how well it has been planned and organized. When you participate in a race there seems to be nothing to it, but in actual fact many, many hours of preparation and work have gone into the planning and execution of the layout.

Let us start at the beginning. You, together with other members of your club, have decided to stage an orienteering race. First, find a suitable area for the race. It should be a mixture of bush and open fields—preferably away from cultivated land—a combination of hills and valleys broken up by streams and a multitude of trails crisscrossing the terrain.

If the race is going to be held at night, do not pick an area where steep cliffs or bluffs will endanger the lives of the participants.

Find out whether you have to get special permission to use the land.

When the area has been selected, permission granted, and with the most recently printed maps at hand, the course-setter can get to work.

Scan the map for the most challenging control points the area has to offer. Next, determine the length of the race. The following table shows the usual lengths of orienteering races:

Class	Course	Miles	Kilometers	Number of Controls
Beginners	Light	1½ to 2	2½ to 3½	4 — 5
Girls and boys under 15	Medium	2 to 3	3½ to 4½	4 — 6
Women over 21	Difficult	4 to 6	6 to 8	8 — 10
Men over 21	Difficult	5 to 8	8 to 12	8 — 10

Careful planning and efficient organization are the keys to a successful orienteering meet.

How and where the controls are placed is vital. Your aim is to give the participants a variety of difficulties to solve, each one different and requiring different methods of reaching the control points. The actual placing of the control points depends on what class of orienteer you are catering to—obscure and hard-to-find control points for the experts, more prominent points for the less experienced. Bear in mind when laying out a course that a control should never be found by chance but should depend solely on the skill of the orienteer.

After determining the control points, draw tentative lines between the controls and study the effect you have created. Have you given the participants enough of a choice of routes? Have you created any doglegs? In other words, have you created a situation whereby a late starter could benefit in finding the control by seeing others leaving that particular control on their way to the next one?

Are the routes far enough away from a handrail? Nor should a control be placed close to a catching feature such as a large lake or a river or a road, where a rough bearing on the compass and no map reading will take the orienteer to the control. If an object such as this is chosen, the control should be placed several hundred feet on the near side to force the participant to make full use of his knowledge of map and compass reading.

Avoid laying a course in a district where serious hazards exist, such as deserted mines with boarded-up mineshafts. Even if the law requires the mineshaft to be boarded up, many years may have elapsed since this was done. The boards may have rotted and the surrounding area may have grown over with underbrush and small trees. Nor should a route take the runner into an area where he can become mired in a bog or quicksand or where there is a possibility of falling rocks. Enough accidents happen without asking for them.

Remember, too, to have a catcher's mitt in order to give the participants a safety bearing and a safe way out.

The course setter, together with the official who is in charge of placing the control markers on "D Day," now takes to the field and walks the whole course. As the officials move along the chosen route they make a thorough check of the map against nature. They carefully plot the spot that has been chosen for each control marker, so that no error will be made in placing the controls. A spray can of paint to mark trees helps

If you are the organizer of an orienteering meet, remember to place the control markers in their proper places at the last possible moment, in order to prevent anyone from getting a sneak preview.

ensure that the actual place of the control is well marked. The marker *must* be in the right place. There is nothing more frustrating than participating in a race only to find that a control has been misplaced after you have spent much time trying to find it. Check and double check the location of the control. Place the control markers in their proper places at the latest possible moment—preferably on the morning of the race—to prevent anyone from getting a sneak preview.

People of all ages and degrees of ability can have fun in an orienteering meet.

As the course setter you also make a check at each control point to see if your description of the control on the description card corresponds to the actual natural feature. At this time, if necessary, make the description more accurate. A simple and easy-to-read description, cutting out all the frills but nevertheless giving a complete and accurate description of the control point, will be appreciated by all participants. (See page 152 for sample descriptions.)

After you have visited and checked out all the controls the stage is set for your orienteering meet. Go ahead and issue the invitations.

INVITATIONS

Send out invitations 30 to 90 days before an important meet, so as to give the participants time to plan their schedules.

The invitations should contain the following information:
- [ ] Nature of the event (cross-country, relay, score, etc.)
- [ ] Date and hour of the event
- [ ] General area of the event and all map information
- [ ] Class divisions and course lengths for different classes
- [ ] Last date for entries
- [ ] Entry fee and whether it includes cost of map
- [ ] Name and address of organizing club or organization
- [ ] Where to send entries
- [ ] If out-of-town entries are expected, state what accommodation is available, together with cost of accommodation

(See page 149 for sample invitations.)

As soon as the entries arrive, the secretary of the organization confirms the receipt of the entries and sends a control card to the participants.

After the race.

After the closing day for entries, hold a draw to determine the starting order. The closing date should be set at least two weeks prior to the meet. After the draw, the secretary sends out a reminder of the meet, including each participant's starting number and starting time. (See page 151 for sample confirmations.)

146

All participating officials meet at the starting area at least two or three hours before the race. The official in charge of the control markers sets out to place the controls in their proper positions; starters ready the starting area; the recorder and time-keeper check the recording lists to make sure that the master maps are properly marked and that enough maps are available for all participants, that description cards are in place and properly marked; the official in charge of the catcher's mitt organizes the safety patrols.

The only thing left to do is wait for the first participant to arrive. Because of your careful planning, you can expect to have a successful meet.

APPENDIX ONE

BULLETIN

The Cambridge Orienteering Club is holding its annual fall
CROSS-COUNTRY ORIENTEERING EVENT, open to members and
non-members on Saturday, November 11, 1979.

AREA:	North of the town of Havelock. Participants will be informed of actual starting point two weeks before events.
EVENTS:	White course, approx. 2-4 miles, for beginners. Red course, approx. 6-10 miles for men over 21. Yellow course, approx. 5-6 miles for women over 21.
FIRST START:	10:30 a.m.
ENTRY FEE:	Seniors $2.00, Juniors $1.25. Includes map.
ACCOMMODATION:	Motel in the town of Havelock. Rooms: single $15.00, double $25.00. Hotel in the town of Havelock. Rooms: single $10.00, double $15.00.
ENTRIES:	Before October 28, 1979, to B. Smith, Secretary, 178 River Road N. Cambridge, Ohio

APPENDIX TWO

CAMBRIDGE ORIENTEERING CLUB'S ANNUAL FALL ORIENTEERING RACE

DATE:
Saturday, November 11, 10.00 a.m.

MEET:
Take Hwy. 30 North in the town of Havelock to half a mile north of Hwy. 7. Turn left onto improved dirt road. Proceed to reception area. Park in designated area.

DRESS:
Long pants and raingear.

EQUIPMENT:
Orienteering compass, red ballpoint pen, plastic map cover, wristwatch, bag lunch.

STARTING TIME:
Your starting number is 21 and your starting time is 10.51 a.m. Please report to the registration desk not later than 30 minutes before start.

SPECIAL NOTES:
Exercise care entering dirt road as the road is heavily travelled by gravel trucks. The law prohibits smoking while walking in the bush.

B. Smith, Secretary

CHECK POINT NO: 1 CONTROL LETTER (H)

Bench Mark 5653 approx. 1,300 yards or 1,200 meters SSE.

CHECK POINT NO: 2 CONTROL LETTER (A)

Track-Trail Crossing approx. 2,600 yards or 2,400 meters SSW.

CHECK POINT NO: 3 CONTROL LETTER (P)

Trail Bend approx. 2,900 yards or 2,650 meters WNW.

CHECK POINT NO: 4 CONTROL LETTER (P)

Track Bend approx. 2,100 yards or 1,900 meters N.

CHECK POINT NO: 5 CONTROL LETTER (Y)

Hill Top approx. 2,055 yards or 1,850 meters E.

CHECK POINT NO: 6 CONTROL LETTER (X)

Gravel Pit approx. 1,800 yards or 1,625 meters ENE.

Examples of control descriptions placed at individual controls

GLOSSARY

AGONIC LINE   An imaginary line on the earth's surface where the declination is zero.

AIMING MARK   An easily identifiable feature in the field not shown on the map and used by the orienteer to follow a bearing.

BACK READING   Reverse reading of the compass done to check the previous aiming point.

BASE PLATE   The rectangular plate on which the compass housing is mounted.

BEARING   Direction, relative position.

BEADBAND   A string of peas or beans, used as an aid for counting double steps.

CARDINAL POINTS   The four main points on the compass: north, east, south, and west.

CATCHER'S MITT   A long, prominent feature in the field, such as, for example, a road, hydro line, river, which acts as a safety device to catch an orienteer if he overshoots his goal.

CATCHING FEATURE   A long feature crossing one's direction of travel.

CHECK POINT   A prominent land feature used by the orienteer to check his progress along his route.

COMPASS   An instrument with a magnetized needle which aligns itself with the earth's magnetic field.

COMPASS, CONVENTIONAL   A compass generally enclosed in a watch-type case.

COMPASS, ORIENTEERING   An instrument combining the magnetic needle and a protractor.

CONTOUR INTERVAL   Distance measured vertically between one contour line and the next.

CONTOUR LINE   An imaginary line in the field combining all points with the same elevation over mean sea level.

CONTROL   One of the several points in the field that the orienteer has to visit in the course of an orienteering race, marked on the master map with a red ring, in the field with a prism-shaped red-and-white marker.

CONTROL CARD   A card carried by the participant in an orienteering race, marked at each control with a different symbol or mark.

CONTROL DESCRIPTION   A card or sheet describing the control to be visited.

CONTROL PUNCH   A pin punch placed at the control and used by the participant to mark his control card.

CROSS-BEARING   A method to determine exact location by using two prominent land features at least 40° apart.

CROSS CHECK   A prominent feature in the field that crosses one's route.

CULTURAL FEATURES   Man-made landscape features: roads, buildings, hydro lines, etc.

DECLINATION   The horizontal angle between the direction of true north and magnetic north, variable according to geographical location.

DIRECTION   Course pursued by a moving body toward a pre-set point or goal.

DIRECTION-OF-TRAVEL-ARROW   The arrow marked on the base plate of the orienteering compass.

GRID   A system of numbered squares printed on a map for locating points by means of a system of coordinates.

HANDRAIL   A long sweeping land feature running in the general direction taken by the orienteer.

HOUSING   The part on the orienteering compass which houses the compass needle, usually fluid-filled to stabilize the needle.

HYDROGRAPHIC FEATURES   All water features, lakes, rivers, streams, swamps, etc.

HYPSOGRAPHIC FEATURES   All elevation features, hills, valleys, etc.

INDEX POINTER   A distinctly marked line or dot on the base plate of the orienteering compass.

INTERCARDINAL POINTS   The four points between the cardinal points: north-east, south-east, south-west, north-west.

ISOGONIC LINE   A line on a map connecting places indicating equal angles of magnetic declination.

LANDMARK   A prominent feature in nature not marked on the map, for example, a large rock or tree.

LATITUDE   Any given point's angular distance on its meridian, north or south of the equator.

LEG   The portion of terrain to be negotiated between controls.

LOADSTONE   A mineral with magnetic properties used by the early seafarers to indicate direction.

LONGITUDE   Any given point's angular distance east or west of the prime meridian running over the old observatory in Greenwich, England.

MAGNETIC LINES   *See isogonic lines.*

MAGNETIC NORTH POLE   A point in northern Canada where all the isogonic lines convene into a point or circle.

MAP   From the Latin word "mappa" meaning cloth, napkin, sheet. A reduced representation of a portion of the earth's surface.

MAP SYMBOLS   Small symbols used by map-makers to indicate features in the landscape.

MASTER MAP   A map on which the controls of an orienteering meet are marked.

MERCATOR, GERHARDUS   A Flemish cartographer and geographer who lived in the late 1700's.

MERCATOR'S PROJECTION   Representation on a plane surface of (or any part of) the surface of the earth, in which the points of the compass preserve the same direction all over the map.

MERIDIAN   A great circle of the earth passing through the poles and any given point on the earth's surface.

ORIENTATION   A method to determine one's location in the field with the help of landscape features, map, or compass, or all three combined.   .

ORIENTEER   A person who is engaged in the art of land navigation with the help of map and compass.

ORIENTEERING   A word borrowed from the Swedish meaning navigation on land with the help of map and compass.

ORIENTING ARROW   An arrow or lines engraved in the bottom of the compass housing of an orienteering compass.

ORIENTING A COMPASS   Holding the compass in such a way that the direction of its dial coincides with the direction in the field.

ORIENTING LINES OF THE COMPASS   Lines running parallel to the orienting arrow in the bottom of the compass housing.

ORIENTING A MAP   Placing the map in a north-south direction to correspond with the features in the field.

PACE   One double step.

PACE COUNTING   Measuring distance in the field by counting double steps.

PACE SCALE   A unit of land graduated in feet or meters where each individual can calibrate distance by counting double steps over a distance of 110 yards or 100 meters.

PARALLELS   Continuously smaller circles towards the poles running parallel to the equator. There are 90 circles on the northern hemisphere and 90 circles on the southern hemisphere.

PROTRACTOR   An instrument for measuring angles, usually in the form of a graduated semicircle.

QUADRANGLE   A rectangular piece of land depicted on a map.

ROMER GAUGE   An instrument graduated in tens and used to determine location on a map with a rectangular grid.

ROUTE   The course between two controls.

SCALE   The relative dimension, the ratio of reduction in a map. The proportion between a distance on a map and the actual distance in the field.

STEERING MARK   An easily identifiable feature in the field.

STELLA POLARIS   The North Star.

TOPOGRAPHIC MAP   The detailed, accurate description of land transferred to a map sheet, a representation on a map of natural or artificial features.

UNIVERSAL TRANSVERSE MERCATOR PROJECTION   The new map-making system where the 36 segments run from pole to pole instead of, as in the earlier system, the segments being taken along the meridian. All measurements are taken from the date line.

INDEX